MY FAVORITE

MARYLAND

RECIPES

Avalynne Tawes

MY FAVORITE

MARYLAND

RECIPES

TIDEWATER PUBLISHERS
CENTREVILLE, MARYLAND

LIBRARY OF CONGRESS CATALOGING-IN-PUBLICATION DATA

TAWES, AVALYNNE, B. 1898
    MY FAVORITE MARYLAND RECIPES / AVALYNNE TAWES.
    P. CM.
    ORIGINALLY PUBLISHED: 1ST ED. NEW YORK : RANDOM HOUSE, 1964.
    INCLUDES INDEX.
    ISBN 0-87033-500-6 (PBK.)
    1. COOKERY, AMERICAN   2. COOKERY—MARYLAND.   I. TITLE.
    TX715.T22   1997
    641-59752—DC21
                                                    96-54735
                                                        CIP

MANUFACTURED IN THE UNITED STATES OF AMERICA

FIRST EDITION PUBLISHED BY RANDOM HOUSE, 1964. FIRST TIDEWATER
PUBLISHERS PRINTING, 1997

Dedicated

to the Memory of

the Two Women Who Inspired Me & Taught Me

to Prepare Many of These Maryland Recipes

My Mother

MINERVA AMERINTH GIBSON

&

My Mother-in-Law

ALICE VIRGINIA TAWES

TABLE

OF CONTENTS

Introduction

Dr. William H. Wroten, a history professor at Salisbury Teachers College, had this to say about the Eastern Shore of Maryland:

"It's been said that the Lord made the earth in six days and rested on Sunday. On the eighth day, He made the Eastern Shore."

Dr. Wroten went on to say that the Eastern Shore "is the only distinct region in the United States known simply as 'The Eastern Shore.' "

Dr. Wroten noted that the early explorers visited this region, early churchmen planted seeds that bore fruit, and politicians, artists, lawyers, military men, farmers, inventors and poets from this region left their mark on history.

I am in complete agreement with Dr. Wroten that "we should make an effort to preserve this way of life."

It is history that people in Maryland have always lived well. That has been a sort of blessing that came, built-in, with our land. As early as 1608, Captain John Smith, the explorer, commented that "if Providence were designing an ideal place for men, it would produce the Chesapeake Bay country." Later, in 1666, one of Lord Baltimore's colonists, writing home to encourage other people to emigrate, exclaimed, "They need not look for any other terrestrial paradise."

These people had no patriotic pride. They were newcomers, open-mindedly looking things over—that is how they felt. Today, we Marylanders certainly do not claim that we live in "paradise," but we are aware that we have inherited some traditions that make our lives distinctively agreeable. One of these is our Maryland foods.

For a hundred years, certain of our specialties have been famous. In the great days of society-with-a-capital-S, no dinner was adequately elegant unless it included our diamondback terrapin. On the more democratic level, fried chicken was "Maryland fried" everywhere. Maryland beaten biscuits, Maryland spoonbread, Lady Baltimore cake—these were some of our State's delicacies that carried their fame beyond our State's borders.

But it has been only recently that the full glory of Maryland food—not just a few dishes—could be generally known. That was because many of our finest food products were perishable.

Now, however, with air transport and freezing, it is possible for us to send our most delicate specialties all over the world. From Government House, Annapolis, I have despatched Maryland terrapin soup, ready to serve, to Sir Winston Churchill in his country home in England.

Also on a special occasion, the Junior Chambers of Commerce of Baltimore, San Francisco and Paris, sat down simultaneously to a traditional "feast" of Maryland fresh crabs, conversing with one another by radio as they ate. Our commercial food packing plants, moreover, are shipping practically all over the world.

Such developments have stirred mixed feelings in people who are concerned with Maryland cookery. We are happy at the spread of specialties. But we also want our culinary art to remain just that—an art.

I was concerned about this myself. I married when I was seventeen, and I have been a Maryland homemaker ever since. I had a normal Eastern Shore girl's knowledge of Maryland cookery, and I got it the way most Maryland girls do—by inheritance. My mother knew the old recipes. She taught them to me.

As the years passed, and changes took place in kitchen equipment and ideas of diet, I realized that the fabulously rich dishes of the past were becoming out of harmony with modern life. Women were counting costs—and calories. They were interested in saving time and space.

Since I love to cook, and, above all things, love my State's characteristic cookery, I thought about this a great deal. In time, I turned the thought into my avocation.

I set about experimenting. I wanted to see if the traditional Maryland deliciousness could be preserved with modern methods. (My husband, once Governor of Maryland, has always been in public life. In those years he held the offices of Clerk of the Court and Comptroller.)

I helped him in his campaigning every way I could, but, when I had time, I worked on my own project—in my kitchen. The result was that, to my astonishment, I produced what politically experienced people have called a "piece of campaign literature."

It was a cookbook, nothing more.

It contained just twenty-two recipes and not a word about politics. Or about anything except food. Yet Mr. Tawes' friends assured me that it had been very helpful in his campaign for the governorship. I am still amazed at that.

I have never sold the book. I had it privately printed and meant to distribute it just among my friends. But news of it spread and I was overwhelmed with requests for copies. Since then, by demand, printing has followed printing. This showed me that, politics aside, many women, like myself, wanted recipes for traditional Maryland dishes that could be prepared in modern kitchens and still keep their traditional excellence. So I went on with my experimenting.

The basic conclusion I have reached is simply this—it is not the mere lavish use of rich ingredients that produces excellence, but an appreciation—precise, intense and respectful—on the part of the cook, of the individual flavor of the food being prepared. That flavor is the material of your art, and that you must know how to handle.

The glory of Maryland food is that it contains an extraordinary number of flavors that are exquisite and individual—

oysters, crabs, terrapin, clams, poultry, hot breads, game and fish.

I am offering here in this book recipes which surely will bring you much joy in good eating.

HORS D'OEUVRES

SPICY PICKLE DIP

(GOOD WITH LOBSTER)

*Makes enough dip for one 10-ounce can
of lobster, drained and boned*

---

1 cup sour cream	1/4 cup chopped parsley
1/3 cup sweet pickle relish, drained	1 teaspoon onion salt
	salt and pepper

☞ Combine all ingredients and mix well.

DIP SAUCE À LA RUSSE

(FOR SHRIMP)

Makes enough for 1 pound of shrimp

½ cup catsup	1 tablespoon Lea and Perrins Sauce
1 tablespoon vinegar	½ teaspoon salt
2 tablespoons lemon juice	1 tablespoon grated onion
2 tablespoons horseradish	1¼ cups mayonnaise
3 good dashes Tabasco	

☞ Mix ingredients together and chill overnight. Do not stir when you empty sauce into serving bowl.

SHRIMP SPREAD

Serves 15 to 20

---

1 cup finely diced cooked shrimp	¼ teaspoon salt
1 tablespoon lemon juice	2 tablespoons finely chopped celery
2 tablespoons sour cream	½ teaspoon sugar
3 tablespoons mayonnaise	

☞ Beat all ingredients together until well blended and smooth. Spread on crackers or toast strips.

If a dip is required, add to the above recipe ½ cup of sour cream and ¼ cup of whipping cream. Put all ingredients in a bowl and beat with electric beater until stiff. Place in center bowl of hors d'oeuvres tray and surround with potato chips or toast triangles. Can be refrigerated till the next day.

CURRY DIP

Makes 1 cup

½ cup mayonnaise	dash red pepper or cayenne
½ cup sour cream	
1 teaspoon curry powder	1 teaspoon lemon juice

☞ Mix together all ingredients. Use as dip for vegetables or seafood.

AVOCADO DIP

Makes 3 cups

1 cup mashed avocado pulp	dash Worcestershire sauce
½ pound package cream cheese	1 tablespoon finely chopped or grated onion
3 tablespoons lemon juice	½ teaspoon salt

☞ Gradually blend avocado pulp into cream cheese until smooth. Add remaining ingredients and mix. Serve as a dip with crackers or potato chips.

CREAM CHEESE COMBINATIONS

Each of these 3 recipes should make 18 portions

Cream Cheese and Olive Spread for White or Cheese Bread

1 4-ounce package cream cheese	dash Worcestershire sauce
10 large stuffed olives	2 tablespoons sour cream
1 tablespoon olive-pickling liquid	1 tablespoon milk

☞ Let cream cheese reach room temperature, place in bowl and add the finely chopped olives, olive liquid, Worcestershire sauce, sour cream and milk. The mixture should have spreading consistency. Spread on crackers or toasted bread strips. Garnish top with olive slices. Same recipe may be used with chopped parsley, and then garnish with tiny spray of parsley.

Cream Cheese and Chive Spread for Whole-Wheat Bread

1 4-ounce package cream cheese	2 tablespoons mayonnaise
2 tablespoons chopped fresh chives	1 tablespoon milk
	dash salt

☞ Let cream cheese reach room temperature, place in bowl and add the other ingredients. Mix well. Let stand for two or three hours before spreading. If mixture becomes too thick to spread, add a little cream so that mixture will spread well.

This spread is nice on whole-wheat bread squares or thin whole-wheat crackers. Two drops of green food coloring will give a spot of color and interest to the spread. Garnish with tiny slice of pickled onion.

Cream Cheese and Nut Spread for Brown Bread

1 4-ounce package cream cheese	1 teaspoon lemon juice
1/4 cup chopped walnuts or pecans	2 tablespoons sweet cream
	2 drops red coloring

☞ Let cream reach room temperature, place in bowl and add other ingredients. Stir well and spread on thin sliced squares of brown bread. Garnish with whole nuts.

COCKTAIL MEATBALLS AND FRANKS
Serves about 20

1 pound ground beef	1 bottle chili sauce
salt and pepper	1 can (or bottle) beer
fat for frying	1 pound large frankfurters

☞ Form seasoned ground beef into small balls. Brown quickly in shortening. Can be deep-fat fried or fried in a heavy frying pan. Add chili sauce and beer. Simmer slowly for 45 minutes. Add frankfurters, cut into 1-inch slices, and cook 15 minutes longer. Serve in chafing dish. This dish may be reheated or frozen successfully.

CHICKEN-LIVER APPETIZERS

Serves about 20

---

1 pound chicken livers	flour
salt and pepper	10 strips bacon

☞ Wash chicken livers in cold water and remove any membrane. Cut livers in half if they are large. Sprinkle with salt and pepper. Then roll in the flour until liver is well covered; sprinkle with more salt and pepper. Cut bacon strips in half and roll around the livers, securing ends with toothpick. Place in broiler tray and broil until brown on one side and then turn to brown on the other, about 4 minutes on each side. Serve hot.

CRAB MEAT BALLS

Makes 30 to 40 balls

---

1 pound cooked fresh	1 unbeaten egg
crab meat	1 tablespoon finely
½ stick soft butter	chopped parsley
salt and pepper to taste	cracker meal or cracker
1 teaspoon horseradish	crumbs
mustard	fat for frying
¼ cup mayonnaise	

☞ Remove all shell from crab meat. Place all ingredients except crumbs and fat in bowl and mix well. Form into small balls and roll in cracker meal or crumbs. Fry in hot deep fat

until golden brown. Drain on absorbent paper and serve hot
pierced with colored toothpick in each ball.

SHARP CHEESE AND ONION SPREAD

Serves 6

---

1 cup grated sharp ched-	2 tablespoons sour cream
dar cheese	2 tablespoons mayonnaise
1 small onion, chopped	2 tablespoons evaporated
very fine	milk, warmed

☞ When cheese is at room temperature, combine with
other ingredients and mix until smooth enough to spread on
crackers. Garnish with very crisp tiny bits of bacon.

HOT OLIVE-CHEESE PUFFS

(FREEZE AHEAD, IF DESIRED)

☞ Blend 1 cup grated natural sharp cheese with 3 tablespoons soft butter or margarine. Stir in ½ cup sifted all-purpose
flour, ¼ teaspoon salt, ½ teaspoon paprika. Mix well. Wrap 1
teaspoon cheese dough around each of 24 stuffed olives, completely covering olive. Bake at 400° ten to fifteen minutes or
until golden. Serve warm.

If desired, wrap olives with cheese dough and freeze. To
serve, take puffs directly from freezer, unwrap frozen puffs
and arrange on ungreased cookie sheet. Bake as indicated
above.

SOUPS

Terrapin

This food has suffered from its fame. People think of it as requiring a professional chef, and professional chefs have tried to add to their reputations by inventing new recipes for terrapin. However, while this went on in cities, Eastern Shore Marylanders were cooking diamondbacks in their kitchens just as a matter of course, and they thought of terrapin as just another good thing to eat. The recipe in this book, an old one, is basic. It can be used for soup, or, with less milk and cream, in pastry shells for a luncheon dish.

PREPARATION OF TERRAPIN:

Drop the live terrapin into boiling water to cover. Be sure the water is boiling hard. Cover and cook until terrapin is tender—about 1 hour. The test is to stick a fork into the sides. It will go in easily when the meat is done. Pour off the water. As soon as the terrapin is cool enough to handle, remove the top and bottom shells. Scrape shells for any meat that adheres to them. Pull off the legs. There are four quarters of meat on the body—one at the top of each leg. These should come off with the legs. Remove the liver, taking care not to break the bile pocket. Cut the bile pocket out. Chop the liver. Skin the legs and cut off the nails. If the meat is still a bit tough, steam it in a little water. Later add this water to the soup.

MARYLAND DIAMONDBACK TERRAPIN SOUP

Serves 8 to 10

1 stick butter	*3 terrapins, 5 to 7 inches*
2 tablespoons flour	*in length (2 small cans*
1 quart fresh milk	*may be substituted)*
salt and pepper	*½ pint thick cream*
6 hard-boiled eggs, sep-	*½ cup sherry wine (op-*
arated	*tional, to be passed*
	after soup is served)

☞ Melt the butter in good-sized saucepan, blend in the flour, then add the milk, salt and pepper and the hard-boiled egg whites which have been chopped fine, then add the terrapin meat (for preparation see above) as is. Mash the egg yolks and add them to the soup mixture. Simmer until thick. Then add the thick cream. Serve hot. When soup has been served, pass sherry wine to be added by individual. Or just before serving, ½ cup of good sherry wine can be mixed in the soup. Maryland beaten biscuits (page 105) are a delicious addition to this rich soup course. Or saltine crackers may be served.

LOBSTER BISQUE NUMBER TWO

Serves 6 to 8

---

1 can cream of green pea
  soup
1 small can tomato paste
1 pint cream

1 pound fresh-cooked
  lobster, cut in bite-sized
  pieces, or 2 8-ounce
  cans lobster meat
⅔ cup imported sherry
  dash Tabasco

☞ Combine all ingredients and simmer gently for 10 minutes. Milk or cream may be added if finished product is too thick. (Same quantity of back-fin crab meat or shrimp may be used instead of lobster.)

QUICK SEAFOOD BISQUE

Serves 6

---

1 cup cooked seafood—
  crab meat, lobster,
  shrimp, oysters, or any
  desired combination
3 tablespoons sherry
1 can condensed tomato
  soup

1 can condensed pea
  soup
1 can consommé
1¼ cups hot rich milk or
  cream

☞ Soak seafood in sherry for 10 to 15 minutes. Combine tomato soup, pea soup, and consommé in medium-sized saucepan and place over low heat until hot. Slowly stir in the milk or cream and add the seafood. Simmer until steaming hot but *do not boil.*

CRAB SOUP

Serves 6 to 8

1 1-pound can back-fin fresh lump crab meat	1 teaspoon salt
¼ pound butter	⅛ teaspoon pepper
1 quart milk	6 to 8 drops Tabasco sauce
1 tablespoon finely chopped parsley	½ cup cream
2 heaping tablespoons finely chopped celery	2 teaspoons flour

☞ Remove all shell from crab meat. In a double boiler melt butter, add milk, parsley, celery, salt, pepper, Tabasco and crab meat. Heat for about 15 minutes, but do not allow mixture to come to a boil. Mix flour with a little cold water to make a paste. Add to the hot mixture and stir until a little thick, then add cream and stir well. Allow the entire mixture to simmer over the hot water in double boiler for 20 minutes, but do not boil. Stir occasionally and be sure to keep water in the lower part cf double boiler. Serve in bowls with saltines or Maryland beaten biscuits (page 105).

SOFT-SHELL CLAM CHOWDER

Serves 6 to 8

---

1 pint soft-shell clams	salt and pepper to taste
2 medium potatoes, diced	dash red pepper
1 medium onion, minced	½ stick butter
	1½ cups milk

☞ Separate body and neck of clams. Skin and grind the necks. Save the juice of the clams. Put potatoes, onion and seasonings into a kettle containing about 2 cups of clam juice (water may be used). Cook until potatoes are about half done (10 minutes) and add clams (necks and body). Cook about 20 minutes and add butter. When melted, reduce heat, add milk, heat thoroughly (don't let milk boil) and serve.

CLAM CHOWDER

Serves 8 to 10

---

18 large clams, chopped fine	½ teaspoon chopped parsley
2 cups water	salt to taste
1 large onion, chopped	dash pepper
4 medium-sized potatoes	3 tablespoons butter
4 slices crisp fried bacon	2 tablespoons flour
¼ teaspoon celery salt	1 quart milk

☞ Cook the chopped clams and juice in 2 cups water for 10 minutes, then add the chopped onion and the potatoes cut in small blocks and cook until tender, or about 15 to 20 minutes. Add the fried bacon cut in small pieces, the celery salt, parsley, salt and pepper.

In a separate saucepan, prepare a white sauce by melting the butter, stirring in flour, then slowly adding the milk. Cook until sauce thickens. Add this sauce to the clam mixture and simmer for 10 minutes on low heat.

VEGETABLE SOUP

Serves 8

¾ pound soup bone or shin of beef	6 sprigs parsley
fat for browning	¼ head cabbage, chopped fine
2 quarts cold water	¼ cup barley or rice
1 small onion, chopped	5 or 6 carrots, diced
1 teaspoon salt	2 cups green beans
2 cups tomatoes, chopped	1 cup diced potatoes
	½ cup chopped celery

☞ Cut half the meat from bone and brown in fat. Add remaining meat and bone to cold water and allow to stand for 20 minutes. Add browned meat, onion and salt; bring to a boil and simmer 2 hours. Add vegetables and simmer 1 hour longer.

BEAN SOUP

Serves 12 to 14

---

2 *pounds white navy*	*smoked ham hock or 3*
beans	*or 4 strips uncooked*
1 *tablespoon sugar*	*bacon*
salt and pepper	

☞ Cover beans with cold water and soak overnight. Drain and re-cover with water. Add ham hock or bacon. (If bacon is used, remove at end of cooking or before serving.) Add sugar and salt and pepper to taste. Simmer slowly for about 4 hours, or until beans are tender. When beans are half cooked, mash beans several times with potato masher until they are broken. This will thicken soup a little.

MUSHROOM SOUP

Serves 6

---

1 *pound mushrooms*	*spoons water*
½ *cup water*	*salt and pepper to taste*
1 *tablespoon cornstarch,*	1 *cup table cream*
blended with 2 table-	1 *cup milk*

☞ Peel and cut mushrooms in small pieces. Grind stems and add to other mushroom pieces. Add the water. Put into top of a double boiler and cook 1 hour. Add cornstarch, salt and pepper, cream and milk. Cook ½ hour, or until thick.

S E A F O O D

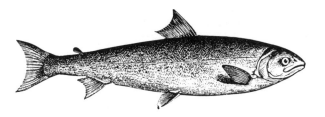

Crabs

I should like to write a great deal about this food, not just because it is so typically Maryland, but because it is so often abused in the kitchen. It has perhaps one of the most delicately delicious flavors of all seafoods, and this flavor furthermore has the quality of being subject to many approaches. Steamed, fried, baked, deviled, or in salad, it lends itself to sensitive preparation. It is too frequently ruined by the unappreciative —crab cannot be enhanced, only complemented.

CRAB MEAT CAKES

(WITH BREAD CRUMBS ADDED)

Makes 8 patties

---

1 1-pound can crab meat	1 teaspoon dry mustard
1 cup rich milk	2 teaspoons Worcester-
1 cup fresh bread	shire sauce
crumbs	3 drops Tabasco
½ teaspoon cayenne pep-	1 egg
per	

☞ Mix above ingredients well—make 8 individual patties and roll in fine, dry bread crumbs. Fry in deep fat until golden brown.

CRAB MEAT CASSEROLE

Serves 8 to 10

---

1 1-pound can crab meat	1 teaspoon olive oil
6 eggs	1 cup cream
salt and pepper	½ cup butter (1 stick)
chopped parsley	1½ tablespoons flour
pinch dry mustard	bread crumbs
1 tablespoon vinegar	

☞ Remove all bones from crab meat; put in large bowl. Boil eggs hard, chop whites; add to crab meat; also add salt and pepper to taste and a little chopped parsley. Mash the egg yolks, add dry mustard, vinegar and olive oil. Mix and add to crab meat. Put flour, cream and butter in a saucepan and cook until thick; pour while hot over crab meat mixture. Mix gently and place in buttered casserole. Cover top with bread crumbs, dot with butter and brown in 350° oven for 20 minutes.

IMPERIAL CRAB NEWBURG CASSEROLE

1 pound back-fin lump crab meat (use the very best)	2 egg yolks
	½ teaspoon salt
	½ teaspoon cayenne
¼ cup butter or marga- rine	1 teaspoon horseradish
	2 tablespoons sherry
2 tablespoons flour	paprika
1 cup cream	

☞ Carefully separate lumps of crab meat and remove any shell or cartilage. Place in a shallow baking dish.

To make sauce, melt butter and add flour, making a smooth paste. Add cream and bring mixture slowly to a boil. Simmer for about two minutes. Add well-beaten egg yolks, salt, cayenne, horseradish and sherry. Cook over low heat for three minutes longer. Pour over crab meat. Sprinkle with paprika and put in 350° oven for about ten minutes.

PERFECT FRIED SOFT CRABS

☞ Clean crabs, salt and pepper them, and dredge heavily with flour. Fry quickly first one side and then the other in 1½ inches of hot fat or 1 inch melted butter, until brown and crisp. Drain on paper towel and serve at once.

CRAB-BURGER

Serves 8

---

1 1-pound can fresh back-fin lump crab meat	1 cup shredded cheese, medium sharp
¾ cup finely chopped celery	1 cup Miracle Whip
2 tablespoons finely grated onion	1 or 2 teaspoons Worcestershire sauce (to taste)
2 tablespoons finely chopped green pepper	1 teaspoon Tabasco
	¾ teaspoon salt
	hamburger rolls

☞ Remove all particles of shell from the crab meat, then combine all the remaining ingredients and mix well. Cut hamburger rolls in half, butter lightly and toast with the buttered side up. (This forms a crisp surface so that mixture will not be absorbed in the bun.) Spread mixture generously on the bun; sprinkle with a little shredded cheese. Place under 400° broiler for 3 to 5 minutes or until light brown and bubbly. Serve hot, immediately.

MARYLAND'S FINEST CRAB IMPERIAL

Serves 4 to 5

---

1 1-pound can of fresh back-fin lump crab meat	pepper
	1 cup heavy mayonnaise
¼ teaspoon salt, dash of	1 beaten whole egg
	dash paprika

☞ Remove all shell from each lump of crab meat. Do this gently so as not to break the lumps. Place crab meat in bowl and add the salt and pepper carefully over all. In another bowl, beat the egg, add the mayonnaise and stir thoroughly. Place enough of this dressing mixture in the crab meat to allow it to stick together. Pack the crab meat mixture lightly in a crab shell for baking (do not pack down, keep light as possible). Try to have a high oval top and cover this top with a thick coating of the dressing mixture. Place in a shallow pan and put in a preheated oven (350-375°) for 30 minutes. Remove from oven and sprinkle top with paprika. Serve while hot.

MARYLAND CRAB CAKES

Makes 8 to 10 cakes

---

1 1-pound can of back-fin lump crab meat, or 1 pound of claw crab meat, or a combination of ½ pound of claw meat and ½ pound of regular grade (*Any of the above combinations can be used with success.*)
2 eggs

2 tablespoons mayonnaise
1 tablespoon Kraft's horseradish mustard
¼ teaspoon salt
⅛ teaspoon pepper
5 drops Tabasco
1 tablespoon chopped parsley
cracker crumbs
fat for frying

☞ Combine all ingredients except crumbs and fat and mix together lightly. Form into desired-size cakes. Do not pack firmly. Prepare cracker crumbs by rolling out saltine crackers into fine crumbs, then pat or roll lightly on the crab cake. Fry in 1½ inches of hot fat in iron frying pan on both sides until a golden brown. Remove and drain on absorbent paper and serve immediately.

DEVILED CRABS
Serves 8

---

1 1-pound can crab meat	1 teaspoon prepared mus-
juice 1 lemon	tard
dash Worcestershire	2 teaspoons milk
sauce	1 cup evaporated milk
dash Tabasco	1 stick butter (1/2 cup)
salt and pepper	6 crackers
2 heaping teaspoons flour	

☞ To crab meat, add lemon juice, Worcestershire sauce, Tabasco and salt and pepper to taste.

To make sauce, mix flour, mustard and milk. Add evaporated milk; cook until thick. Remove from stove and stir in ¾ stick of butter, melted. Pour over crab meat and mix. Pack into shells. Mash 6 crackers and mix with ¼ stick of butter. Sprinkle on top of crabs. Bake in hot oven (375°) for 15 minutes, or until brown.

CRAB CUSTARD
Serves 8

---

1 1-pound can crab	1½ cups milk
meat	¼ teaspoon dry mustard
2 beaten eggs	salt and pepper

☞ To crab meat, add eggs, milk, mustard, and salt and pepper to taste. Place in buttered casserole and top with bits of butter. Bake in 325° oven about 20 minutes, or until set.

Oysters

This is one of the few seafoods that can be eaten raw. Its cookery, therefore, is not directed at changing its flavor, but at giving it variety on the table. Most recipes are simple. However, in every one there is some little thing that *has* to be done. It is these little things that make the difference between perfect oyster cookery and indifference in the finished product. In the recipes that follow, the aforesaid little things are underscored.

FRIED OYSTERS

☞ Wash all grit from 1 pint of oysters. Dry on clean cloth. Beat 2 eggs well. Add ½ cup milk, salt and pepper. Dip oysters in egg batter, then in saltine cracker crumbs. Repeat. Fry both sides in hot deep shortening until golden brown. Drain on paper towel. Serve at once.

MARYLAND OYSTER PIE

Serves 8 to 10

---

1 stick butter	2 teaspoons salt (or to
1 quart fresh oysters	taste)
1 quart milk	dash pepper
2 tablespoons flour and 2	
tablespoons water	
mixed to a paste	

☞ Melt the butter in a 3-quart saucepan. Strain off all the liquid from the oysters and save. Wash oysters thoroughly to remove all grit and add to hot butter. Simmer for 10 minutes, then add the strained oyster liquid and stir. Add milk and continue to simmer. Then stir in flour paste and simmer until thick. Add salt and pepper and pour into a buttered baking dish. Cover top of baking dish with rich oyster crust rolled to ½-inch thickness, prick with fork, dot with butter and bake in hot oven (400°) for 20 to 25 minutes, or until brown.

RICH OYSTER CRUST

---

2 cups flour	1 teaspoon salt
4 teaspoons baking pow-der	6 tablespoons shortening
	¾ cup milk

☞ Sift dry ingredients together and cut in shortening. Add milk all at once to make a soft dough. Place on floured board and knead lightly a few seconds, using as little flour as possible on board. Roll out dough about ½ inch thick and use as instructed above.

OYSTER CROQUETTES

Serves 8

1 cup oysters	2 tablespoons cream
1 cup seasoned mashed potatoes	1 egg
¼ stick butter	cracker crumbs
salt and pepper	fat for frying

☞ Chop oysters very fine, add mashed potatoes seasoned with butter, salt, pepper and cream. Make into croquettes, dip in egg, then roll in cracker crumbs and fry a nice golden brown in hot deep fat.

OYSTER STEW

Serves 4 generously

☞ Melt ¾ stick of butter in heavy saucepan. Wash all grit off 1 pint of oysters. Put into hot butter and let simmer a few minutes. Add salt and pepper to taste. Add a pint of milk; bring to a near boil and serve at once with oyster crackers or saltines.

SCALLOPED OYSTERS

Serves 8 to 10

☞ Drain liquid from 1 quart oysters and save. Wash oysters to remove all grit. Place alternate layers of cracker crumbs and oysters in a buttered baking dish, beginning and ending with crackers. Season each layer with salt, pepper and lumps of butter. Strain oyster liquid and pour over ingredients. Then add sufficient quantity of milk to fill casserole to about 1 inch from top of dish. Bake about 30 minutes in medium oven.

DEVILED OYSTERS IN SHELLS

Serves 8 to 10

1 pint fresh oysters	*dash cayenne*
4 tablespoons butter	*1 teaspoon lemon juice*
4 tablespoons flour	*½ tablespoons finely*
⅔ cup milk, scalded	*chopped parsley*
1 'egg yolk	*fine, dry bread crumbs*
½ teaspoons salt	

☞ Clean, drain and slightly chop the oysters. Make sauce by mixing together and bringing to a boil the butter, flour and milk. Add the egg yolk, salt, cayenne, lemon juice and parsley.

Butter the cleaned and washed oyster shells and arrange on a pan. Half fill with the above mixture and cover with bread crumbs and small pieces of butter. Bake about 15 minutes in a hot oven (400°).

PANNED OYSTERS

Serves 4 to 6

¼ *stick butter*	1 *tablespoon flour*
1 *pint oysters*	*salt and pepper*
2 *cups hot water*	*toast*

☞ Melt butter in heavy skillet. Wash all grit from oysters. Drain. Add oysters to melted butter and cook until oysters are quite brown. (They will stick slightly to skillet.) Add the 2 cups of hot water. Using pancake turner, scrape bottom of pan to loosen brown particles. Cook 5 minutes, stirring constantly. Thicken with the tablespoon of flour which has been mixed with a small amount of cold water. Season with salt and pepper. Serve hot on toast.

STEAMED OYSTERS ON HALF-SHELL

☞ Scrub thoroughly, using a stiff brush, the shells of approximately ½ bushel of oysters. Place oysters in a large shallow pan, not more than 2 layers deep. Add ¼ inch of water. Cook in pre-heated oven at 400° until the oyster shells have partially opened and oysters are slightly brown around the edges. Remove from oven, open oysters, and serve hot. These oysters may be served with cocktail sauce or horseradish sauce. In Maryland, they are often served with side dishes of vinegar which has been seasoned with salt and pepper.

OYSTER-MACARONI BAKE

Serves 8

---

1 quart oysters	1 cup light cream
1 small package elbow macaroni or spaghetti, cooked and drained chopped parsley	salt and pepper bread crumbs

☞ Butter 2-quart casserole. Beginning with macaroni, alternate layers of macaroni, oysters, parsley and seasonings. When casserole is full, pour 1 cup light cream over all. Top with well-buttered bread crumbs. Bake in 350° oven for about ½ hour.

Clams

CLAMS CASINO

Makes about 1 dozen

---

2 dozen clams, ground
4 tablespoons melted but-
ter
2 tablespoons minced
onion
4 slices chopped crisp
bacon

2 tablespoons minced
parsley
2 tablespoons minced
celery
dash Tabasco
salt and pepper to taste
1 cup rolled cracker
crumbs

☞ Mix well all ingredients except cracker crumbs. Place cleaned clam shells in shallow pan. Pack with clam mixture. Top with buttered cracker crumbs. Broil under medium heat until nicely browned. Serve hot.

SOFT-SHELL FRENCH-FRIED CLAMS

Serves 8 to 10

---

1 egg, beaten	1 quart soft-shell clams,
1 tablespoon milk	drained
1 teaspoon salt	2 cups yellow corn meal
2 shakes black pepper	fat for frying

☞ Combine egg, milk and seasonings. Dip clams in mixture and roll in corn meal. Fry in a basket in deep fat (375°) for 3 minutes, drain on paper towel.

DEVILED CLAMS

Serves 8

---

2 cups chopped clams	1 teaspoon salt
½ cup clam liquid	2 hard-cooked eggs,
1 tablespoon minced	finely chopped
onion	4 drops Tabasco
1 tablespoon green	½ teaspoon prepared
pepper	mustard
¼ cup finely chopped	¾ cup cracker crumbs
celery	1 cup buttered bread
5 tablespoons butter	crumbs

☞ Cook clams, liquid, onion, pepper, celery, butter and salt about 6 minutes or until tender. Add remaining ingredients. Fill greased ramekins or cleaned clam shells. Sprinkle with buttered bread crumbs and bake in moderate oven (350°) about 20 minutes, or until a golden brown.

MARYLAND CLAM FRITTERS

Makes about 20 medium-sized fritters

---

25 medium-sized clams	1/4 teaspoon baking powder
1 egg	pepper and salt to taste
4 tablespoons flour	fat or oil for frying

☞ Drain clams slightly and grind. Add egg, flour, baking powder, salt and pepper. Drop by spoonfuls, fry in hot fat or oil about ½ inch deep.

CHESAPEAKE BAY SOFT-SHELL CLAM FRITTERS

Serves 8

---

1 pint clams, fresh or canned	1/2 cup milk
1½ cups flour	salt and pepper to taste
2 eggs	dash of cayenne
2 teaspoons baking powder	

☞ Drain clams and chop them. Beat eggs till light; add milk; sift flour and baking powder and beat into the eggs and milk. Add chopped clams, then add seasonings. Drop mixture into deep, hot fat and fry till golden brown. Drain and serve.

DEVILED SOFT-SHELL CLAMS

Serves 4

---

1 pint soft-shell clams	4 tablespoons butter
2 tablespoons minced onion	3 tablespoons flour
1 tablespoon parsley flakes	1 cup milk
½ cup bread crumbs	salt, black and red pepper to taste

☞ Melt butter, add flour and milk and cook until lightly colored. Chop very fine, or grind, the clams. (I recommend using the neck and body, if available.) Then mix with onion, parsley flakes and bread crumbs. Add enough of the sauce to bind mixture together. Mix in seasonings and fill cleaned clam shells with the mixture. Sprinkle lightly with more bread crumbs and dot with butter. Brown quickly under broiler.

SUPERB STUFFED SHAD

Serves 4 to 6, depending on size of shad

☞ Place 1 large, fresh, boned shad (preferably with roe) in shallow pan which has been covered with long strip of foil. Make pocket in shad for stuffing by slicing back the skin from the flesh. Stuff this with back-fin lump crab meat from which all shells have been removed. Stuff space where backbone of shad has been removed with mashed roe (either fresh shad roe or herring roe). Cover fish with slices of onion. Lay strips of bacon over all. Season with salt and pepper with dots of butter. Fold foil gently over fish and bake in moderate oven for 1 hour.

FRIED CHESAPEAKE BAY
SOFT-SHELL CLAMS
Serves 25

---

6 pounds (3 quarts)   salt and pepper to taste
  shucked clams (use   frying fat
  only the body)   pancake flour

☞ Drain clams, salt and pepper to taste (use salt moderately). Roll the clams heavily in the pancake flour, place in basket of deep fryer and submerge in deep hot fat. Fry at 375° for 1½ minutes. If necessary, shake the basket during frying time to prevent the clams from sticking together. Drain on absorbent paper and serve very hot.

"CHEAP AND EASY" CLAM IMPERIAL
Serves 5

---

25 clams   1 ounce butter
1 pint half-cream—half-   1 egg yolk
  milk   1 tablespoon sherry
1 tablespoon flour   ½ cup bread crumbs

☞ Drain clams. Run through grinder, or chop until *very fine*. Make a creamed sauce with milk, flour, butter, egg yolk. Add the sherry. Put clams in baking dish or casserole. Add the sauce. Sprinkle with bread crumbs. Bake in moderate oven (375°) about 20 minutes, or until golden brown.

SEAFOOD A LA KING

Serves 10 to 12

6 tablespoons butter	1½ cups cooked seafood,
1 cup sliced mushrooms	drained, in large
6 tablespoons flour	pieces
1 teaspoon salt	½ cup slivered green
⅛ teaspoon pepper	pepper
2½ cups milk	¼ cup slivered pimiento
	buttered toast points

☞ Melt butter; cook mushrooms in butter for 10 minutes. Remove from stove. Blend in flour, add salt and pepper. Slowly add milk, stirring constantly. Continue to cook, stirring until smooth and thickened. Gently stir in seafood, green pepper and pimiento. Serve on buttered toast points.

SHRIMP NEWBURG

Serves 8

2 tablespoons butter	1 pound cooked shrimp
1¾ tablespoons flour	salt
1 cup cream	paprika
3 tablespoons tomato	cayenne
catsup	3 tablespoons sherry
¾ tablespoon Worcester-	
shire sauce	

☞ Melt butter. Stir in flour until blended. Stir cream in slowly. When sauce is thick, stir in tomato catsup and Worcestershire sauce. Add the shrimp and stir until heated and thick. Season with salt (sparingly), paprika, few grains of cayenne. Immediately before serving, add sherry. Serve in patty shells.

HOLIDAY TUNA LOAF

Makes 12 servings

---

8 ounces wide noodles	2 teaspoons salt
6 shelled hard-cooked eggs, quartered	⅛ teaspoon pepper
1 13-ounce can tuna fish, coarsely flaked, drained	2 teaspoons bottled thick meat sauce
½ cup minced onion	2 tablespoons lemon juice
½ cup pickle relish	2 cups canned condensed chicken broth, undiluted
1 cup cooked fresh mushrooms	2 cups milk
⅓ cup butter, margarine, fat or salad oil	1 5-ounce package potato chips, crushed
2 tablespoons flour	

☞ Cook and drain noodles. Add next 5 ingredients. Melt butter, add flour and seasonings. Stir in liquids and cook, stirring constantly until thickened. Add sauce to noodle-tuna mixture. Grease pan (13″ by 9″). Spread thin layer of crushed potato chips over bottom. Put in half the noodle-tuna mixture, then a sprinkling of chips, remaining mixture, then chips. Store in refrigerator 24 hours. Bake in moderate oven (375°) for 45 minutes. Cut into 12 squares.

LOBSTER IN SHELLS
Serves 2

1 boiled lobster	2 tablespoons chopped
cream	pimiento
½ cup sherry	salt and pepper
speck cayenne	speck of mace
½ cup sautéed mush-	brown buttered crumbs
rooms, sliced	paprika

☞ Open lobster, split claws and remove all meat from claws and body. Cut up meat, put into a frying pan, and cover with cream. Add sherry and cayenne. Cook the cream down to a sauce consistency. Add mushrooms and chopped pimiento. Season with salt and pepper and mace. When the sauce is reduced to a good consistency, fill the cleaned shells with the mixture. Garnish with brown buttered crumbs, paprika, lobster claws and mushrooms.

DELICIOUS CRISP-
FRIED FISH ROE
Serves 4

1 pint fish roe (herring,	2 cups flour
shad or trout can be	1 stick butter, more if
used)	necessary
1 teaspoon salt, or to taste	
dash of pepper	

☞ Wash the roe in cold water, remove membrane blood veins but not the thin casing; add salt and pepper. Spread flour in shallow pan and roll the roe individually very thoroughly in flour until they are white. Have iron frying pan on stove with hot melted butter (not hot enough to burn). Place the roe evenly in the hot butter; watch and turn until brown on all sides. Do not leave the stove until the tender roe is golden brown on all sides. Do not overcook, but be sure roe is crisp. Remove to paper towel for only a couple of seconds and then serve while piping hot and crisp.

FISH BALLS

Serves 6

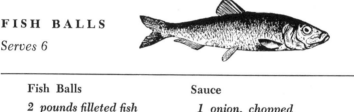

Fish Balls	Sauce
2 *pounds filleted fish*	1 *onion, chopped*
1 *large onion*	1 *carrot, chopped*
2 *stalks celery*	2 *stalks celery with*
few sprigs parsley	*leaves, cut up*
salt and pepper to taste	½ *small can tomato sauce*
1 *tablespoon flour*	*salt and pepper to taste*
	water

☞ To make fish balls, chop fish, onion, celery, and parsley, and mix together well. Form mixture into balls and sprinkle with salt, pepper, and flour. Set aside while making the sauce. Fill a medium-sized saucepan one-fourth full of water. Add sauce ingredients, and boil over medium heat for 15 to 20 minutes. Reduce heat to low and slowly add fish balls to sauce. Simmer for one hour. Cooked shrimp, mushrooms, or oysters may be added to sauce for variation. Serve with broad noodles.

SHRIMP IN TIMBALES

Serves 8 to 10

4 tablespoons butter	1 cup cooked or canned
4 tablespoons flour	shrimp
2 cups milk	1 cup cooked peas
1 teaspoon salt	timbales or toast
⅛ teaspoon pepper	

Melt butter; blend in flour; then stir in milk gradually. Stir constantly over low heat or hot water until smooth and thick. Add salt, pepper, shrimp and peas. Cook until shrimp are heated through. Serve in timbales or on toast.

SCALLOPS AU GRATIN

Serves 6 to 8

1½ pounds scallops	dash white pepper
3 tablespoons butter	2 cups milk
3 tablespoons flour	½ cup bread crumbs
1 teaspoon salt	½ cup grated store cheese

Sauté scallops in butter, over moderately low heat, for about 15 minutes, stirring frequently to lightly brown all sides. Remove scallops to a buttered baking dish. Stir flour and seasonings into the butter in which scallops were sautéed. Add milk and cook until the sauce thickens. Pour the sauce over the scallops. Top with combined crumbs and cheese and bake at 350° for 20 to 25 minutes.

FRIED FISH (WITHOUT GREASE)

¾ cup corn meal	flour
½ cup water	½ teaspoon salt
1 tablespoon butter	fish fillets or steaks (1
1 egg	fillet per person)

☞ Mix corn meal and water. Melt and add butter, add egg and mix thoroughly. Roll fish first in flour to cover well, then in above mixture. Place in frying pan heated to 250° and brown both sides in open pan. Do not crowd the pieces. After browning, put all the pieces in a covered pan and let cook until done—slowly, about 30 minutes at 350°.

This recipe calls for a roaster with ventilator.

BLUEFISH BAKED TO PERFECTION

Serves 4 to 6

1 large bluefish, 3 to 5	salt, pepper and a little
pounds	onion, or large onion, ac-
⅓ cup melted butter	cording to taste
	juice of half a lemon

☞ Split the fish down the back, wipe it well and lay in a greased pan. Melt the butter and add the salt, pepper, onion and lemon juice, and pour a little of the mixture over the fish.

Place in a hot oven and bake about ¾ of an hour, basting with the prepared butter every 10 minutes. Serve very hot, with or without a sauce.

BOILED TROUT

(MARYLAND STYLE)

Serves about 4

---

2 *good-sized trout*	4 *strips bacon*
3 *teaspoons salt, or more*	2 *hard-cooked eggs,*
if desired	*sliced*

☞ Cut the fish in half and remove the backbone. Sprinkle each piece with salt. Add the salt to approximately 1½ quarts of water or enough to cover the fish well. Put fish pieces in the water and allow to boil for 15 to 20 minutes, or until the fish is tender but will still hold together. Remove carefully from water and place on platter, meat side up. While fish is cooking, cut the bacon strips in pieces and fry slowly. The hot grease should be poured over the fish as soon as it has been put on the platter. Decorate with the bacon curls and slices of egg. If trout is not available, rock fish, flounder, or fresh mackerel can be used.

POULTRY

A SPECIAL MARYLAND WAY
WITH WILD DUCKS

Serves 8

☞ Soak 1 pair plucked and drawn ducks overnight in strong salt water. Pour off salt water and rinse thoroughly. Place in large kettle and cover with fresh water. Add salt to taste, 2 strips of bacon and 1 small onion. Simmer on top of stove, uncovered, until water has been reduced to one-third. Cover and continue cooking until ducks stick to bottom of pan and brown. Remove from pan and rub ducks with butter. Wild goose can be cooked successfully this way also.

ROAST PHEASANT WITH STUFFING

Serves 4

1 pheasant, 3 to 3½ pounds	salt, pepper, and flour
3 tablespoons butter	1 cup water

☞ Clean pheasant and wipe with a damp cloth. If stuffing is desired, fill cavity with Pheasant Stuffing and close by sewing or skewers. Spread butter over breast and legs and sprinkle bird with salt, pepper, and flour. Add 1 cup of water to bottom of roasting pan. Place pheasant on back in pan. Bake at 450° for 15 minutes. Reduce oven heat to 350°, and cook until breast is tender. Baste every 10 minutes, adding water if necessary. Turn bird occasionally to brown evenly.

PHEASANT STUFFING

2 tablespoons butter	½ cup potatoes, diced and parboiled
1 small onion, diced	
½ cup celery, diced	1 egg, beaten
4 cups bread cubes	1 teaspoon parsley, minced
½ teaspoon salt	
⅛ teaspoon black pepper	milk to moisten

☞ Melt butter, add onion and celery, and sauté over low fire. Add to bread cubes, mix, and then add all other ingredients together with enough milk to barely moisten. Mix lightly with a fork. Use to stuff pheasant.

OVEN-FRIED CHICKEN

Serves 6

☞ Melt a stick of butter. Add salt and pepper. Salt 6 chicken breasts lightly and dip in butter. Have ready crumbs made from 1 box Rice Krispies rolled very fine with rolling pin. Roll chicken in crumbs and lay in shallow pan on foil paper. Bake in oven, uncovered, 1 hour at 350°. Serve at once.

EASTERN SHO' BAR-B-Q CHICKEN

Serves 8

☞ Start with two 2½-pound broilers, split. Dip the chicken in barbecue sauce and place on grill. Turn chicken over every 10 minutes and baste with the sauce. Cooking time from 1 to 1¼ hours, depending on size of chickens.

S a u c e : (enough for six halves)
½ pint cooking oil
½ pint cider vinegar
2 tablespoons salt
¼ teaspoon pepper
1½ teaspoons poultry seasoning
1 well-beaten egg
4 drops Tabasco
¼ teaspoon paprika

☞ Mix dry ingredients. Add liquids, then egg. Mix well.

CHICKEN MOUSSE

(RICH, UNUSUAL AND DELICIOUS!)

Serves 8 to 10

2 tablespoons Knox gelatin	½ teaspoon lemon juice
¼ cup cold water	½ cup chicken aspic jelly
½ cup hot chicken broth	½ cup almonds, chopped
1 pint cold chopped cooked chicken	6 tablespoons mayonnaise
1 teaspoon salt	¼ teaspoon paprika
1 teaspoon onion juice	1 cup whipping cream
	2 heads lettuce

☞ Soak gelatine in cold water for 5 minutes. Then dissolve in hot chicken broth. Add all other ingredients together, except cream and lettuce, and mix well. Set aside to cool. Whip cream and fold into cool mixture. Pour into mold. Chill. Unmold and serve on lettuce.

OLD MARYLAND FRIED CHICKEN

Serves 6

1 2½- to 3-pound young chicken, cleaned and drawn	2 teaspoons salt
1 cup flour	½ teaspoon pepper
	1 cup lard

☞ Wash chicken and cut in pieces for frying. In a brown paper bag mix the flour, salt, pepper, add chicken; twist top of bag securely and shake until chicken is well covered with the flour mixture. Melt lard in iron frying pan and heat over moderate heat. Place chicken in the hot fat and fry until chicken is tender and golden brown, turning continuously. Drain on absorbent paper. Serve while hot.

OLD-FASHIONED CHICKEN PIE

Serves 8 to 10

1 3-pound chicken, or larger if desired	¼ teaspoon pepper
	½ teaspoon celery seed
1 quart or more of water	2 tablespoons flour
2 teaspoons salt	½ stick of butter

☞ Place chicken in kettle on top of stove and cover with water. Add salt, pepper and celery seed, cover and let boil until chicken is tender enough to fall off the bone.

Remove chicken from liquid stock and let cool, then take the meat from the bones and place in a well-buttered baking dish.

To the chicken liquid stock add flour mixed into a paste with a little cold water, then stir and let cook until thickened. Add the butter and mix well, salt and pepper to taste.

Pour this mixture over the chicken in the baking dish. There should be sufficient to almost fill the dish. If not, add some milk, approximately a cup. Then cover with the crust as described below and bake in a 375° oven for 20 minutes or until the crust is brown.

RICH CRUST

2 cups flour	1 teaspoon salt
4 teaspoons baking	6 tablespoons shortening
powder	¾ cup milk

☞ Sift the dry ingredients together and cut in the shortening. Add milk all at once so as to make the dough soft. Place on a floured board and knead lightly, using as little flour as possible on the board. Roll dough out about ½ inch thick and place over the baking dish filled with chicken and thickened sauce. Pinch edges firmly around the dish, prick center of dough with fork, dot with butter. Bake as directed in above recipe.

CHICKEN CROQUETTES

Serves 4 to 6

2 level teaspoons flour	14 ounces boiled chicken,
½ pint milk	chopped fine
1 teaspoon salt	egg
pinch red pepper	fine, dry bread crumbs
½ pound butter	fat for frying

☞ Mix the flour smooth in a little of the milk. Put the rest of the milk in top of a double boiler; when scalded, pour in the flour mixture. Stir in the salt, pepper and butter. When slightly thickened, mix it with the chicken and set aside to cool. Then make into croquettes, dip in egg and roll in bread crumbs. Fry in hot deep fat.

CREAMED CHICKEN IN PATTY SHELLS

Serves 8 to 10

---

1 tablespoon butter	2 cups cooked chicken
1 tablespoon flour	(cut in small pieces)
(heaping)	½ cup cream
1 pint (2 cups) milk	salt and pepper to taste
	2 hard-cooked eggs

☞ Melt butter in saucepan on low heat; add flour and mix to a paste. Stir in milk gradually, add chicken, cream, salt and pepper, egg yolks mashed fine; then add egg whites cut up in small pieces. Cook on low heat until thick. Serve hot in patty shells.

CHICKEN SALAD

Serves 6

---

3 cups diced cold	3 sweet pickles, chopped
chicken	1 cup mayonnaise
1½ cups diced celery	lettuce
1 teaspoon salt	capers
4 hard-cooked eggs	olives

☞ Combine chicken, celery and salt. Cut 3 eggs in pieces and add with pickles. Blend with mayonnaise. Serve on lettuce and garnish with capers, slices of egg, and olives. See page 65 for wonderful dressing for this salad, or top with additional mayonnaise.

CHICKEN SOUFFLÉ

Serves 6

---

2 tablespoons butter	dash nutmeg
4 tablespoons flour	4 eggs, separated
½ cup chicken broth	1½ cups chicken, cut fine
1 cup evaporated milk	½ cup coarsely cut
¼ teaspoon salt	almonds

Combine and cook first 4 ingredients into thick sauce. Season with salt and nutmeg. Remove from heat and beat in egg yolks one at a time. Set over boiling water and cook 3 minutes longer. Fold in chicken and almonds, then stiffly beaten egg whites. Turn into buttered baking dish, set in pan of water. Bake in moderate oven (350°) until set, about 40 minutes. Almonds may be left out if desired. Serve hot or cold.

SHERRIED CHICKEN

Serves 4

---

1 2½-pound chicken	1 medium onion, thinly
salt and pepper	sliced
garlic salt	¼ cup tomato sauce
¼ cup butter	¼ cup sherry
	½ cup water

☞ Cut chicken into quarters. Season and sauté in butter until golden brown. Remove chicken and arrange in single layer in shallow pan (skin side down). Add onion to butter in skillet. Cook until limp, not brown. Add liquids and mix well. Pour half of this sauce over chicken. Bake at 375° for ½ hour. Turn chicken, add remainder of sauce, bake ½ hour longer. Baste occasionally. Serve with rice and spiced fruit. For festive touch, sliced mushrooms or toasted slivered almonds may be added near end of cooking time. This chicken may be reheated or frozen.

BROILED BONELESS CHICKEN
ON SMITHFIELD HAM
WITH MUSHROOM GRAVY

Serves 6

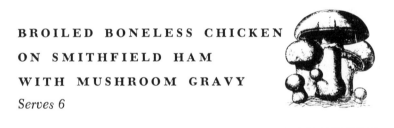

6 chicken breasts	6 slices toast
salt and pepper	6 slices Smithfield ham
¼ pound butter	

☞ Remove bone from chicken breasts. Sprinkle with salt and pepper. Melt butter, dip seasoned chicken pieces into butter, and place on rack in broiling pan. Broil for approximately 10 to 15 minutes on each side in preheated broiler about 5 inches from heat. When chicken is tender, remove from broiler. Place 6 slices of toast on a serving platter. Top each slice of toast with a slice of Smithfield ham, and top each slice of ham with one broiled chicken breast. Pour mushroom gravy over all. Garnish as desired.

MUSHROOM GRAVY

½ pound fresh mush-
rooms
¼ pound butter
1 tablespoon flour
¼ cup cold water

1½ cups chicken stock, or
canned chicken broth
salt and pepper to
taste

☞ Remove stems from mushrooms, wash, slice, and sauté in butter for approximately 5 minutes over low heat or until tender and slightly browned. Add flour to cold water and stir until smooth. Add stock to mushrooms and then add the flour and water mixture. Bring to a boil over medium heat, season with salt and pepper, and cook for 8 to 10 minutes or until mixture has thickened.

CAPON BREAST, BROILED, WITH SMITHFIELD HAM AND ORANGE SAUCE

Serves 4

☞ Have butcher bone a 5-pound capon. Remove skin from breast and divide breast into four pieces. Roll each piece into a ball shape and fasten ends with a skewer. Rub pieces with butter and sprinkle with salt and pepper. Place in broiling pan, lined with aluminum foil. Broil 4 inches from flame in preheated broiler for 20 minutes on each side, or until tender and lightly browned.

Arrange four slices of toast on a serving platter. On each slice of toast, place a slice of Smithfield ham, and on top of ham, place one portion of broiled capon. Pour orange sauce (page 71) over all and garnish with slice of orange. Decorate platter with orange slices and parsley. Serve hot.

SMALL CAPON
WITH BING CHERRY SAUCE

Serves 4

Have butcher bone a 5-pound capon. Remove skin from breast and divide breast into four pieces. Roll each piece into a ball shape and fasten ends with a skewer. Rub pieces with butter and sprinkle with salt and pepper. Place in shallow baking pan, containing about ¼ inch of water. Melt one stick of butter and pour over fowl. Place sheet of aluminum foil loosely over top of pieces of breast and bake in preheated 350° oven for 1½ hours, basting frequently to keep moist. Add more water if needed for basting. Serve with cherry sauce.

BING CHERRY SAUCE

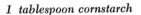

1 tablespoon cornstarch	½ lemon (juice only)
½ cup cold water	¼ stick butter
1 1-pound can of Bing cherries	1 cup water
	dash salt
1½ teaspoons sugar	

Add cornstarch to ½ cup cold water and stir until smooth. Pour cherries into medium-sized saucepan, add the cornstarch, and mix well. Add the sugar, lemon juice, butter, cup of water, and salt. Cook over medium heat for about 10 minutes or until sauce is thickened and clear. Bright red pie cherries may be used as a substitute for Bing cherries. If red pie cherries are used, add an additional teaspoonful of sugar. Serve hot.

STUFFED BAKED TURKEY
WITH GIBLET GRAVY
(MARYLAND STYLE)

14- to 16-pound turkey	*2 teaspoons pepper*
(and giblets and neck)	*¼ pound butter*
2 tablespoons salt	

First start cooking giblets in salted water until tender. Cut into small pieces. Select a thick-breasted turkey, wash inside and out with cold water. Rub a tablespoon or more of salt thoroughly on the inside of the turkey and an equal amount on the outside. Also sprinkle and rub with pepper. Then rub the outside of the turkey with softened stick of butter or butter substitute.

Stuff the inside of the turkey with dressing, made as follows:

20 slices white bread	*¼ teaspoon sage*
½ cup chopped celery	*¼ teaspoon thyme*
leaves	*cup or more of liquid*
¼ pound melted butter	*left from cooking gib-*
salt and pepper	*lets*
20 saltines	

Toast bread in oven very brown, grate or roll bread into crumbs and small pieces. Add celery leaves, butter, salt and pepper to taste, and saltines rolled into small pieces. Sprinkle with sage and thyme and mix well. Moisten with liquid left from cooking giblets. Stuff the mixture into the turkey cavity. Place the bird in a roasting pan with ½ inch of water in bottom, cover and cook in slow oven (325°) 4 hours or until tender, basting every half hour during the baking. Remove browned turkey from roasting pan.

Giblet gravy can be made by adding 3 cups of hot water to the essence in the roasting pan. Then stir in 3 tablespoons of flour that has been mixed with 1 cup of cold water into a paste. Add the cut-up giblets and more salt if needed, cook until thickened.

M E A T S

MARYLAND-COOKED MUSKRAT

Should serve 8 to 10

---

2 *cleaned fresh muskrats*	1 *small onion, sliced*
2 *teaspoons salt*	4 *strips salt bacon or salt*
½ *teaspoon pepper*	*fat pork*
3 *to 4 tablespoons flour*	½ *teaspoon sage*
½ *cup bacon fat*	

☞ The muskrats should be soaked overnight in salted cold water (about 1 tablespoon salt to enough water to cover the meat). Then boil in clean salted water for 15 to 20 minutes. Remove from heat and water. Cool and remove head. Cut remainder of muskrat into portions like a frying chicken. Sprinkle each piece with a little salt, pepper and flour, and fry in bacon fat which has been heated in a heavy Dutch-oven type of roasting pan or saucepan. Turn meat until brown on all sides. Then add sufficient water to cover the meat and also add onion slices and the four slices of bacon, 2 teaspoons salt, ½ teaspoon pepper and the sage. Cook slowly for two hours or until all the water has cooked down and meat is dry and browned a little.

If gravy is desired, add a cup of cold water mixed with 1 tablespoon flour to pan after removing meat. Scrape bits from pan and cook until thick and hot.

R O A S T   L E G   O F   L A M B

Serves 10

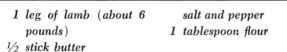

1 leg of lamb (about 6 pounds)	*salt and pepper*
	1 tablespoon flour
½ stick butter	

Trim the skin from the leg of lamb, leaving as much fat as possible. Rub all sides with butter and sprinkle with salt, pepper and flour. Place in roaster with ½ inch of water in the pan. Bake in oven, uncovered, at 375° with meat thermometer until desired doneness. Garnish with fresh mint leaves and serve hot. For a second meal, serve cold and sliced thin. Always serve with mint jelly.

BAKED HAM SLICE

Serves 4

---

1 2-pound ham slice ¾" thick	½ cup brown sugar
2 tablespoons prepared mustard	12 whole cloves

☞ Place ham in a shallow pan. Moisten with prepared mustard. Pat on brown sugar. Stick cloves in fat. Cook about 1 hour at 350° or until tender.

SMITHFIELD HAM

Allow ½ pound per serving

---

1 10- to 12-pound Smith-field or country-cured ham	¼ cup vinegar
1 cup brown sugar	2 tablespoons prepared mustard

☞ Completely cover ham with water and soak for 24 hours. Pour off water, add fresh water, and scrub ham with a stiff brush, removing as much of dark coating as possible. Do not remove the skin at this time. Place ham in large kettle of water and bring water to a boil. Reduce heat to simmer and let cook for 4 hours or until tender when tested with a fork. Allow ham to cool in the water in which it was cooked. When cool, remove from kettle and peel off the skin, leaving some fat on the ham. Place ham in shallow baking pan. Make a paste of brown sugar, vinegar, and mustard. Spread paste over ham and bake uncovered in preheated 350° oven for 30 minutes or until glazed and slightly browned. Ham should be allowed to cool and then be refrigerated for a few hours before slicing. Ham should be sliced very thin for serving. May also be served hot, if desired.

MEAT LOAF WITH A NEW TASTE

Serves 4 to 6

1 egg	½ teaspoon prepared
½ cup milk	mustard
1 tablespoon finely	1 cup soft bread crumbs
grated onion pulp and	(crusts removed)
juice	1 pound ground beef
1 teaspoon salt, and pep-	chuck
per to taste	4 hard-cooked eggs
1 teaspoon Worcester-	
shire sauce	

☞ Beat the egg lightly; mix with milk, onion, salt, pepper, Worcestershire, mustard and bread crumbs; allow to stand about 5 minutes. Mix in beef. Pack half of meat mixture into loaf-size buttered baking dish (about 8-by-4-by-3″); arrange the 4 whole hard-cooked eggs lengthwise over meat in zigzag fashion; pack in remaining meat mixture. Bake in moderate oven 50 to 60 minutes. Allow to stand for about 5 minutes. Turn out and slice.

MEAT LOAF

Serves 6 to 8

1½ pounds ground meat (⅔ beef, ⅓ pork)	1 small onion, chopped
1 #2 can tomato soup	½ cup cracker meal, or corn flakes
2 sticks celery, chopped	3 beaten eggs
½ cup catsup	salt and pepper to
½ green pepper, chopped	taste

☞ Mix all ingredients. Shape in a loaf. Place in greased pan with cover. Bake at 400° about 1 hour, or until firm and brown. Remove from pan. Add 2 tablespoons flour to juice which cooked from loaf; add 1 cup hot water; boil until it thickens. Serve this gravy over sliced meat loaf.

STUFFED BEEFSTEAK

Serves 4

---

2 pounds or more of round steak, cut 2″ thick	stuffing as for turkey (page 50)
salt and pepper	butter

☞ Season steak with salt and pepper, spread thick with the stuffing, fold together and sear the edges. Put bits of butter on top. Place in a pan with a little water for basting. Bake at 350°. Keep covered the first ½ hour. Uncover and bake ½ hour longer, or until tender.

QUICK SKILLET DINNER

Serves 4 to 6

---

1 pound ground beef
   oil
1 tablespoon instant
   minced onion
½ cup tomato sauce

1 cup cooked spinach
4 eggs
   pinch oregano
   grated Parmesan cheese

☞ Brown beef in small amount of oil. Combine minced onion with tomato sauce. Stir into meat, along with spinach, beaten eggs and oregano. Combine all ingredients and cook, stirring until eggs are set. Sprinkle with Parmesan cheese and serve with hot garlic bread.

BARBECUED BEEF

Serves 8

---

1 5-pound roast (chuck, brisket or any cut desired)
2 teaspoons salt
1 teaspoon celery seed

1 clove garlic (or ¼ teaspoon garlic powder)
1 bottle barbecue sauce
2 tablespoons brown sugar

☞ Combine salt and celery seed and rub meat well on all sides. Sear meat under broiler until brown on all sides. Place in Dutch oven and add garlic, barbecue sauce, and brown sugar. Cover with tight-fitting lid and roast in 300° oven for one hour or until very tender. Slice and serve.

BEEF À LA STROGANOFF
Serves 8

2 *pounds sirloin tip, cut in strips*	1 *large onion, chopped*
2 *tablespoons French dressing*	1 *small can bouillon*
butter, margarine, or bacon fat	½ *cup red wine*
½ *pound sliced mushrooms*	1 *teaspoon lemon juice*
	salt and pepper
	flour
	¼ *to* ½ *cup sour cream*

☞ Marinate sirloin strips in French dressing for ½ hour. Brown at medium heat, in butter, margarine or bacon fat for about 5 minutes. Remove from pan. Add more fat to pan, if necessary, and sauté mushrooms and the onion, until onion is golden brown. Return meat to pan. Add next 4 ingredients. Cover pan and cook over low heat until tender—from 45 to 60 minutes. Thicken a little with flour blended with water. Just before serving, blend in sour cream and simmer a few minutes (do not boil). If more liquid is desired, add wine and water.

EASY CHEESEBURGERS
Serves 10

2 *pounds ground beef*	½ *pound sliced American cheese*
1 *package onion soup mix*	*toasted buns*
salt and pepper to taste	

☞ Combine ground beef, onion soup mix and salt and pepper. Shape into patties. Broil or charcoal broil to desired brownness. Top with slices of cheese and heat until melted. Serve on toasted buns.

VEAL LOAF

Serves 8

1 pound ground veal	4 tablespoons milk
1 pound ground pork	lump of butter size of
½ cup cracker crumbs	walnut
(salted)	strips of bacon

☞ Mix well all ingredients except bacon. Shape into loaf. Bake in a shallow pan in 350° oven for about 1 hour with strips of bacon underneath and across top of loaf. Serve hot or cold.

MEAT SUBSTITUTES

STUFFED PANCAKES

Serves 6

¾ cup flour	3 eggs separated
1 teaspoon sugar	1 cup thin white sauce
¾ teaspoon salt	grated Parmesan cheese
1¾ cups milk	

☞ Sift flour, sugar and salt into bowl and add ¾ cup milk gradually. Add egg yolks. Beat hard for 4 minutes. Pour in remaining milk while beating. Then fold in stiffly beaten whites. Fry cakes size of a saucer in a buttered griddle. In middle of each cake, place 1 teaspoon filling.

Filling:

⅓ pound mushrooms	1 teaspoon chopped celery
1 teaspoon minced onion	
3 tablespoons butter	salt and pepper
1 tablespoon flour	1 cup cold chicken or veal,
¾ cup broth or gravy	coarsely chopped
1 teaspoon chopped parsley	

☞ Slice mushrooms. Fry with onion in butter. Add flour, moisten with broth, season with parsley, celery, salt and pepper. Add meat. Cook 2 minutes. Place one teaspoon in center of each cake as directed above. Roll cakes into small cylinders, cover with white sauce (page 69). Dust lightly with cheese. Brown under hot broiler and serve.

BEAUREGARD EGGS

Serves 5

5 eggs	1 tablespoon cornstarch
1 cup milk	5 squares toast
butter size of walnut	salt and pepper to taste

☞ Boil eggs 20 minutes; chop whites fine, rub yolks through a sieve. Do not mix them. Boil milk, butter, and cornstarch together, remove from stove and add the egg whites, salt and pepper. Place toast on hot dish, cover with layer of hot sauce, then sprinkle on layer of egg yolks. Salt and pepper to taste.

STUFFED EGGS
Serves 3

---

6 *eggs*
1 *tablespoon chopped*
  meat, cooked (chicken
  or ham)
1 *teaspoon chopped pars-*
  ley
salt and pepper to taste

1 *tablespoon butter*
  flour
1 *beaten egg*
  fine cracker crumbs
  lard for frying

☞ Boil eggs hard, about 10 minutes; peel and put in cold water to cool. Cut in halves, and mash yolks fine. Add to yolks the chopped meat, parsley, salt, pepper and butter. Mix all together and stuff into the egg halves. Stick 2 halves together and rub with flour. Brush with beaten egg, roll in fine cracker crumbs and fry in deep hot lard until golden brown.

DRESSINGS
SAUCES
CONDIMENTS

CHEF'S SALAD DRESSING FOR FRUIT

Enough for 6 or 8 salads

---

1 cup mayonnaise

3 tablespoons sour cream

1 teaspoon sugar

2 teaspoons fruit juice
(fresh fruit or pineapple
juice)

☞ Blend or whip the above ingredients together.

SOUR-CREAM DRESSING

(FOR CUCUMBERS)   *Makes about 2 cups*

1 cup thick sour cream	1 teaspoon salt
1 tablespoon minced on-ion	pinch black pepper
	2 tablespoons sugar
2 tablespoons vinegar	⅓ cup mayonnaise

☞ Blend all ingredients thoroughly. Cover and store in refrigerator until ready to use.

Preparation of cucumbers:

Slice and soak in cold salt water 20 minutes. When ready to serve, drain and toss with Dressing.

HONEY DRESSING

(ESPECIALLY GOOD ON FRUIT SALAD) *Makes 2 cups*

⅔ cup sugar	⅓ cup strained honey
1 teaspoon dry mustard	5 tablespoons vinegar
1 teaspoon paprika	1 tablespoon lemon juice
¼ teaspoon salt	1 teaspoon grated onion
1 teaspoon celery seed	1 cup salad oil

☞ Mix dry ingredients, add honey, vinegar, lemon juice and onion. Add oil slowly, beating constantly at high speed with electric mixer.

EASY BUT DELICIOUS DRESSING

(FOR POTATO SALAD OR CHICKEN SALAD)

Makes about 1½ pints

---

3 unbeaten eggs	1 teaspoon salt
1 tablespoon dry mustard	dash of celery salt
2 tablespoons flour	½ cup vinegar
(rounded)	1 cup water
6 tablespoons sugar	½ pint mayonnaise
(heaping)	

☞ Combine all ingredients, except mayonnaise, in a heavy medium-sized saucepan. Beat with a rotary egg beater until well mixed. Place over medium heat and, stirring constantly, cook until thick. Remove from stove and stir in the mayonnaise. Let cool before mixing salad. Can be stored in the refrigerator for a week or more.

TOSSED-SALAD DRESSING

Makes 1 quart

---

1 pint salad oil	juice from 2 lemons
1 bottle catsup	3 medium-sized onions,
1¼ cups sugar	ground
½ teaspoon salt	⅔ cup vinegar

☞ Mix all ingredients together or shake in tight jar. Pour over salad, toss lightly.

EASY GOVERNMENT HOUSE DRESSING

Makes about ½ pint

½ cup white vinegar	1 teaspoon salt
⅓ cup vegetable oil	sugar to taste

☞ Mix ingredients well. When ready to serve salad, pour dressing over and toss lightly.

SAUCE FOR SHRIMP

Makes 1¼ cups

---

1 cup catsup	dash Worcestershire
¼ teaspoon horseradish	few drops lemon juice
(or to taste)	sugar to taste

☞ Mix ingredients thoroughly.

TARTAR SAUCE

---

1 cup mayonnaise	1 small onion, finely
1 large chopped dill	chopped
pickle	dill pickle juice
1 tablespoon chopped	
parsley	

☞ Mix the pickle, parsley, and onion with the mayonnaise. Thin to desired consistency with pickle juice. Serve cold.

TARTAR CREAM SAUCE

(FOR SEAFOOD)

⅔ cup evaporated milk	2 tablespoons drained
¼ cup mayonnaise or	pickle relish
salad dressing	1 tablespoon finely
	chopped onion

☞ Mix all ingredients in a 1-quart saucepan. Stir over medium heat to thicken. Do not boil. May be served hot or cold.

HOLLANDAISE SAUCE

Makes 4 servings

½ cup butter	¼ teaspoon salt
3 egg yolks	pinch of cayenne
2 tablespoons lemon	
juice	

☞ Heat the butter to bubbling in a small saucepan. Place the egg yolks, lemon juice, salt and cayenne in the container of an electric blender. Cover and turn motor on low speed. Immediately remove the cover and pour in the hot butter in a steady stream. When all the butter is added, turn off the motor.

CHEESE SAUCE

Serves 10

¼ pound butter	2 cups milk
4 tablespoons flour	1 cup grated sharp cheese
¼ teaspoon salt	

☞ Melt butter in saucepan over low heat and add flour and salt. Add milk slowly, stirring constantly. Then add grated cheese and continue to cook over medium heat until sauce is thick and smooth.

DELICIOUS STEAK SAUCE

Serves 8

---

1 bottle Cross & Blackwell Meat Sauce	1 teaspoon English mustard (dry)
¼ bottle A-1 Sauce	about ¾ cup light cream
1 tablespoon Worcestershire sauce	salt and pepper
juice of ½ lemon	

☞ Mix all ingredients well. Add light cream until light brown color is obtained. Bring all to a boiling point. Remove from heat and pour over broiled steaks. Sauce can also be used over hamburgers. Remaining sauce can be kept in glass container in refrigerator.

THICK WHITE SAUCE

½ stick butter   1 cup cream or milk
2 tablespoons flour

☞ Melt butter and stir in flour; add cream or milk. Cook and stir until thick.

GENUINE MARYLAND BAR-B-Q SAUCE

(FOR OUTDOOR COOKING)

Enough for 8 servings

¼ cup melted butter   ¼ teaspoon fresh ground
2 tablespoons lemon   pepper
    juice   1 teaspoon grated orange
½ teaspoon orange ex-   rind
    tract   1 tablespoon dark black
¼ teaspoon Tabasco   molasses
1 teaspoon monosodium   1 tablespoon brown
    glutamate   sugar
1 teaspoon salt

☞ Mix all ingredients well and heat over charcoal fire while waiting for flames to die down. Coat meat or poultry with sauce before placing on grill. Continue basting while cooking. Meat should cook slowly so it will be tender and juicy on the inside, properly cooked on the outside.

DELICIOUS CHOCOLATE SAUCE

Serves 10 or 12

---

3 squares unsweetened chocolate	1 large can evaporated milk
½ stick butter	1 teaspoon vanilla
3 cups sugar	¼ teaspoon salt
	6 large marshmallows

☞ Melt chocolate and butter together in top of double boiler. Add sugar and evaporated milk alternately, one half at time, and stir constantly until sauce thickens (about 15 to 20 minutes). Add vanilla and salt and beat in marshmallows.

SUZETTE SAUCE

Makes 6 servings

---

2 egg yolks	½ teaspoon salt
½ pound sweet butter	1 orange, juice and rind
1 cup powdered sugar	

☞ Mix all ingredients. Cook in double boiler until thick. If you desire to serve flaming, pour ½ cup hot brandy over sauce and light when ready to serve.

SAUCE FOR ANGEL-FOOD CAKE OR ICE CREAM

Makes 6 servings

☞ Combine ½ cup dark or golden seedless raisins with 1 cup firmly packed brown sugar and 3 tablespoons butter. Heat until sugar dissolves. Slowly add ½ cup light cream and 1 teaspoon vanilla. Heat 1 minute longer. Serve warm or cold.

ORANGE SAUCE

(FOR ROAST FOWL)

Enough for 10 to 12 servings

½ stick butter	shredded rind from 1 medium orange
⅛ teaspoon salt	
2 tablespoons cornstarch	juice of 2 medium oranges
1 cup water	
1 tablespoon honey	8 very thin slices of orange
1 cup concentrated stock from fowl	

☞ Melt butter in top of double boiler, add salt and cornstarch and the cup of water, stirring until smooth and clear. Then add all remaining ingredients except orange slices. Cook about 20 minutes. Before ready to serve, add the orange slices and cook another 10 minutes.

This sauce can be used successfully over servings of roast pheasant, quail, wild duck, wild goose or capon. Spoon sauce over individual servings and be sure an orange slice is placed on each serving.

WHOLE-CRANBERRY SAUCE

Serves 10

---

1 quart cranberries
1½ cups water

2 cups sugar

☞ Boil cranberries and water together for 6 minutes. Add sugar and let come to boil again. Boil 3 minutes. Pour into molds. Chill and unmold on plate when ready to serve.

CREAMY FUDGE-NUT SAUCE

Makes about 2 cups

---

3 squares unsweetened
chocolate
½ cup light cream
¾ cup sugar
3 tablespoons butter or
margarine

dash salt
¾ teaspoon pure vanilla
extract
½ cup chopped walnuts
or pecans

☞ In a 1-quart saucepan combine chocolate and cream. Set over low heat and stir constantly until chocolate is melted and mixture is smooth and blended. Add sugar, butter and salt. Cook, stirring constantly, 3 to 5 minutes longer, or until slightly thickened. Remove from heat, add vanilla and nuts. Serve warm over waffles topped with vanilla or coffee ice cream.

BRANDY SAUCE

Makes 4 generous servings

2 cups water	1 tablespoon cornstarch
1/4 stick butter	1 teaspoon vanilla
4 tablespoons sugar	4 tablespoons brandy,
1/8 teaspoon salt	rum or sherry

 Heat water and butter, add sugar and salt. Dissolve cornstarch in 1/4 cup cold water, then stir into hot mixture and let come to a boil and thicken. Add vanilla, cook 5 minutes. Remove from heat and add brandy (or rum or sherry). Serve warm over pudding, plain cake or fruit dumplings.

PINK RHUBARB SHERBET

(DELICIOUS AS MEAT ACCOMPANIMENT, ALSO MAY BE USED AS DESSERT) *Serves 8 to 10*

4 cups diced fresh rhubarb	2 tablespoons lemon juice
1/2 cup boiling water	1 teaspoon grated lemon rind
1 cup sugar	1/4 teaspoon salt
1/2 cup light corn syrup	2 tablespoons sugar
1/2 cup orange juice	2 egg whites

Cook rhubarb in 1/2 cup boiling water about 15 minutes. Remove from heat and stir in sugar until dissolved. Then add syrup, orange juice, lemon juice and grated rind and let cool. Add salt and sugar and fold in stiffly beaten egg whites.

Freeze in ice trays, beating several times during freezing (takes about 2 hours). Serve in squares on lettuce for salad, or with whipped cream for dessert.

CURRIED FRUIT BAKE

Makes 12 servings

---

1 #303 can cling peach halves	1/3 cup butter
1 #2 can pineapple slices	3/4 cup light-brown sugar, packed
1 #303 can pear halves	4 teaspoons curry powder
5 maraschino cherries with stems	

Day before:

Preheat oven to 325°. Meanwhile drain fruits; dry well on paper towel; arrange in 1½-quart casserole.

Melt butter; add brown sugar and curry; spoon over fruit. Bake 1 hour, uncovered; refrigerate.

30 minutes before serving:

Reheat casserole of curried fruit in 350° oven 30 minutes. Serve warm with ham, lamb or poultry.

SWEET PICKLED WATERMELON

Makes 10 pint jars

☞ Cut the white rind from average-sized watermelon in 1-inch pieces. Cook in water with ½ teaspoon baking soda until tender. Drain off water, put rind in syrup and simmer for 40 minutes.

Syrup:

4 pounds sugar	1 teaspoon cloves
3 pints vinegar	1 teaspoon cinnamon

☞ Mix syrup ingredients together in saucepan large enough to hold rind pieces when added. Stir ingredients until all are dissolved; bring to a boil, add rind pieces. While hot, pour into hot, sterilized jars and seal. Keeps for a year or more in cold place.

SANDWICH PICKLES

Makes 1 quart

---

1 quart sliced cucumbers	½ teaspoon turmeric
1 pint onions, sliced thick	1 tablespoon mustard
1 heaping tablespoon salt	seed (optional)
1 sliced red pepper	1 tablespoon celery seed
1 sliced green pepper	(optional)
1 teaspoon dry mustard	hot vinegar to cover
1 cup sugar	

☞ Combine cucumbers, onions, and salt and let stand for 24 hours. Pour off liquid, and add red and green pepper, mustard, sugar, turmeric, mustard seed, and celery seed. Place mixture in a saucepan, cover with full strength hot vinegar, place on stove, and heat thoroughly. Pour into jars while hot, seal, and store in a cool place.

MAMA'S CHOW CHOW
(WONDERFUL!)

Makes 12 pints

¼ bushel green tomatoes (about 18 pounds)	1 head cauliflower, cut up fine
14 onions	small box white mustard seed
12 sweet peppers (6 red, 6 green)	1 box celery seed
1 cup salt	2 tablespoons dry mustard
2 quarts cider vinegar	1 tablespoon allspice
4½ pounds sugar (9 cups)	1 tablespoon cloves
1 1-pint jar sweet pickles, cut up fine	1 teaspoon turmeric

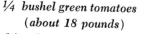 Cut or chop tomatoes, onions and sweet peppers fine. Put in large basin. Sprinkle over all 1 cup salt and add water nearly to top. Let this stand overnight.

Next morning:

Drain off all liquid from above mixture. Place in large basin, add the cider vinegar, sugar, sweet pickles, cauliflower, mustard seed, celery seed, dry mustard and spices. Bring to a boil and cook over very moderate heat for 1 hour. When cold, pack into clean jars and seal. Will keep a year or more if kept in a cold place.

S A L A D S

LIME SALAD

(COOL AND DELICIOUS)

Serves 12

---

2 3-ounce packages lime
  flavor gelatin
1 cup boiling water
½ cup pineapple juice
1 cup creamed cottage
  cheese
1 3-ounce pkg. cream
  cheese

1 #2 can crushed
  pineapple (drained)
½ cup chopped nuts
2 tablespoons minced
  pimento
½ cup chopped celery

☞ Dissolve gelatin in boiling water, cool. Add pineapple juice. Whip cottage cheese and cream cheese. Add to other ingredients. Add all ingredients to gelatin. Pour in fancy-shaped mold. Chill. Turn out of mold on bed of lettuce.

CREAM CHEESE SALAD

(THIS SALAD IS AN EASTER DELIGHT —
ESPECIALLY GOOD WITH SEAFOOD OR CHICKEN)

Serves 10 to 12

---

2 packages lemon flavor
  gelatin
4 cups hot water
½ pound package cream
  cheese
1 tablespoon lemon juice

1 #2 can crushed pine-
  apple
½ cup pecans, chopped
2 tablespoons mayonnaise
1 teaspoon green food
  coloring

☞ Dissolve gelatin in hot water. Mix softened cream cheese, pineapple, lemon juice, pecans and mayonnaise. Add to gelatin, after gelatin is *slightly* firm. Add green food coloring. Put into greased mold or individual custard cup molds and chill until firm.

FROZEN SALAD

(DELICIOUS !)   *Serves 6 to 8*

1½ cups pineapple, cut in
  small pieces
1 large can apricots,
  chopped
1 large bottle mara-
  schino cherries,
  chopped

1 cup sugar
2 large packages cream
  cheese
milk
½ cup mayonnaise
1 pint whipping cream
1 cup black walnuts

☞ Combine first 3 ingredients and drain thoroughly. Mix sugar with fruit and let stand for 1 hour. Soften cream cheese with a little milk. Add mayonnaise and beat. Stir this mixture into fruit. Whip cream and fold into fruit mixture. Add walnuts, if desired. Freeze in molds.

DELICIOUS FROZEN FRUIT SALAD

Serves 8 to 10

1 large can white cherries	1 pound marshmallows,
1 large can sliced pine-	cut into small pieces, or
apple, cut into small	use miniature marsh-
pieces	mallows
	juice of 1 lemon

☞ Put the cherries, pineapple and marshmallows into mixing bowl and stir in lemon juice. Let stand in refrigerator while the sauce is being made.

Sauce:

4 egg yolks	¼ teaspoon salt
1 cup evaporated milk	1 cup chopped nuts
¼ teaspoon dry mustard	1 cup heavy whipping cream

☞ Combine above ingredients, except nuts and whipping cream, and cook in top of double boiler, stirring constantly until it thickens. Pour over fruit while hot. Stir thoroughly. Put mixture in refrigerator and chill for 2 hours. Whip the heavy cream and fold into cooled mixture with the nuts. Pour into ice-cube trays and freeze. Cut in squares and serve on lettuce.

CHRISTMAS FROZEN FRUIT SALAD

Serves 6 to 8

---

1 3-ounce pkg. cream cheese
2 tablespoons pineapple juice
⅓ cup mayonnaise
1 cup drained crushed pineapple
2 tablespoons rum or rum flavoring

½ cup glazed red cherries
½ cup glazed green cherries
½ cup walnut or pecan meats
1 cup whipping cream
lettuce

☞ Mix cheese with pineapple juice. Add mayonnaise and mix until smooth. Add crushed pineapple, rum, cherries and nuts. Whip cream until stiff and fold into mixture. Pour into freezing tray and freeze, without stirring. When ready to serve, cut into squares and pile on nests of lettuce.

OLD-FASHIONED POTATO SALAD

Serves 8 to 10

---

8 large white potatoes
2 cups finely chopped celery
4 hard-cooked eggs, chopped

8 small sweet pickles, chopped
1 large onion

☞ Cook potatoes in salted water until tender. When cool cut into cubes, add chopped celery, chopped eggs, and chopped pickles.

Mix all ingredients with Easy But Delicious Dressing (page 65). Peel onion and slice in half. Put in bottom of large bowl and pile potato mixture on top. Onion can be removed before serving. For those who do not care for too much onion, this is fine, but for those who like a lot of onion flavor, onion can be chopped fine and added to salad.

Variations for Potato Salad Recipe

1. For those who do not care for chopped onion in potato salad, try placing onion, which has been peeled and cut in half, in the bottom of the salad bowl and then covering the onion with the potato salad. Remove the onion before serving.

2. The addition of 4 tablespoonfuls of finely chopped sweet pickle to the potato salad ingredients will give the salad a good flavor.

(The idea of putting an onion in the bottom of the bowl of potato salad is one I have used for years. You get the onion flavor but not the odor and taste of onion afterward.)

GOVERNMENT

HOUSE SALAD

☞ Shred head of lettuce in salad bowl. Add tomato wedges, diced celery, sliced radishes, cucumbers and Bermuda onion. Chill thoroughly. Toss with easy Government House dressing (page 66).

SHRIMP-POTATO SALAD

Serves 10

2 cups cooked shrimp, cut up *(leave a few whole)* 3 cups potatoes, cooked and diced	1½ cups chopped celery 2 sliced hard-cooked eggs
Dressing: 1 cup mayonnaise 3 tablespoons prepared mustard	1 tablespoon lemon juice 1½ teaspoon grated onion ⅛ teaspoon pepper

☞ Combine dressing ingredients thoroughly. Pour over shrimp, potato and celery mixture. When ready to serve, garnish with hard-cooked eggs and whole shrimp.

CRAB MEAT SALAD

(EXOTIC CRAB SALAD)   *Serves 5*

☞ This is a unique crab meat salad. You may wish to add other ingredients to enhance the flavor to your particular taste.

6½ ounce can crab meat 1 cup celery, finely cut up 1 cup seedless white grapes	2 hard-cooked eggs, chopped 1 4-ounce can blanched almonds mayonnaise

☞ Have crab meat well chilled. Carefully pull all the small shell pieces out of the crab meat and break into small chunks. To this add celery, grapes, hard-cooked eggs and almonds. Stir in enough mayonnaise to suit taste. Have all ingredients well chilled before mixing and chill again before serving. Mound the crab meat on crisp lettuce leaves. (This same recipe is also excellent when chicken is used in place of crab.)

EASTERN SHORE CRAB SALAD

Serves 6

1 1-pound can of backfin lump crab meat	⅛ teaspoon paprika
1 cup finely chopped celery	½ teaspoon salt
2 tablespoons chopped sweet red or green pimiento (sweet peppers)	3 tablespoons catsup
	1 cup salad dressing
	juice ½ lemon
	½ teaspoon prepared mustard
	1½ tablespoons sugar

☞ Remove all shell and sinew from crab meat, leaving lumps of the same size as much as possible. Place in bowl with celery and green pepper. In another bowl mix all the other ingredients to form the salad dressing mixture. Then mix the dressing with the crab meat being careful to keep the lumps of crab meat whole. Refrigerate until ready to use or serve at once on lettuce leaf.

Garnish suggestions for this salad: sliced hard-cooked eggs or tomato wedges. Or serve the salad in a hollowed-out ripe tomato.

HOT CHICKEN SALAD
Serves 6

2 cups coarsely diced cooked chicken	2 tablespoons lemon juice
2 cups chopped celery	1 cup mayonnaise
½ cup chopped, toasted almonds (*leave a few whole*)	½ cup grated American cheese
½ teaspoon salt	1 cup crushed potato chips

☞ Mix first 6 ingredients. Place in flat casserole measuring about 8 inches square. Mix grated cheese and crushed potato chips and sprinkle lightly over top. Bake in 450° oven for 10 minutes. Serve piping hot.

CHEF'S FRESH FRUIT SALAD
Serves 4

4 lettuce leaves	16 strawberries
16 pear slices, ½ inch thick	16 green seedless grapes
16 peach slices, ½ inch thick	4 sprigs fresh mint
16 grapefruit sections	4 tablespoonfuls cream cheese dressing

☞ Place one lettuce leaf on each of four salad plates. Arrange four slices each of pear, peach, and grapefruit in a fan shape on each lettuce leaf. In the center of each salad, place a heaping tablespoonful of Cream Cheese Dressing and garnish dressing with a sprig of mint. Scatter one-fourth of strawberries and grapes over each salad.

CREAM CHEESE DRESSING

Serves four, or six toppings for fruit salad

1 3-ounce package of Philadelphia cream cheese	1 dash salt
	3 tablespoons red maraschino cherry juice

☞ Combine all ingredients and mix well; then whip until smooth and fluffy.

AVOCADO SALAD AND DRESSING

Serves 12 to 14

3 heads of lettuce
1 large head Romaine lettuce
3 #2 cans grapefruit sections, drained
3 avocados, sliced (add just before serving)

☞ Add dressing—mix and serve in individual or large salad bowl as desired.

Dressing

1 cup salad oil	3 tablespoons sugar
¾ cup vinegar	½ teaspoon salt
	1 teaspoon paprika

☞ Place ingredients in jar and shake well. Pour over salad and toss.

WALDORF SALAD

Serves 6

3 ripe apples	⅓ cup seedless white
½ cup English walnut	cherries
meats	1 tablespoon red mara-
½ cup seedless raisins	schino cherries, cut up

☞ Peel applies and cut into cubes. Cut English walnut meats and combine with raisins (which have been soaked in cold water for at least 1 hour) and white and maraschino cherries. Mix together in bowl and combine with following mixture: 1 cup mayonnaise, 1 tablespoon sugar, 1 teaspoon lemon juice, 1 tablespoon maraschino cherry juice. Mix well and pour over fruit mixture. Chill, serve on lettuce.

KIDNEY BEAN SALAD

Serves 12

(SOUNDS VERY PLEBEIAN BUT REALLY DELICIOUS!)

4 #1 cans red kidney	1 small jar (10-12
beans	ounce) sweet gherkin
2 cups chopped celery	pickles, chopped
1 cup chopped onion	salt and pepper to taste
	½ cup mayonnaise

☞ Mix all ingredients, serve on lettuce or water cress.

COLE SLAW (very good)

Serves 6 to 8

---

1 small head of cabbage (grated medium fine)	1 heaping tablespoon mayonnaise
½ cup brown vinegar	½ teaspoon salt
1 cup sugar	½ teaspoon fine celery seed
¼ cup water	

☞ Heat vinegar, sugar, and water to melt sugar. Place in jar with mayonnaise, salt, and celery seed. Shake well and when ready to serve pour over grated cabbage.

VEGETABLES

OLD-FASHIONED STEWED ASPARAGUS

Serves 6

3 *strips salt bacon*	1 *teaspoon salt*
1 *quart of water*	*dash of pepper, or more*
1 *bunch fresh asparagus*	*if desired*
2 *tablespoons butter*	2 *teaspoons flour*

☞ Boil bacon in 1 quart of water in a saucepan for about 15 minutes, or until the bacon is tender. Have asparagus washed and free from all grit, cut into pieces about 1 inch long. Put cut asparagus into boiling water with bacon and add butter, salt and pepper and let simmer for half an hour. Dissolve the flour in a little water and stir into the stew and let simmer for another 20 minutes. Bacon may be removed or cut into small pieces and served with the asparagus.

STRING BEANS WITH ALMONDS
Serves 8

3 pounds fresh tender string beans	1 teaspoon sugar
1½ teaspoons salt	2 strips bacon
½ teaspoon pepper	½ cup slivered almonds
	¼ pound butter

☞ Wash string beans, remove strings, and break into 2-inch pieces. Place in saucepan and add water just to cover. Add salt, pepper, sugar, and bacon strips. Cook over medium heat for 30 minutes or until beans are tender. While beans are cooking, melt butter in small skillet and stir almonds into butter. Sauté until almonds are lightly browned. Remove beans from stove at end of cooking time, remove bacon strips, and pour off water from pan. Stir in the sautéed almonds. Replace on low heat to keep warm until ready to serve.

CAULIFLOWER AU GRATIN
Serves 6

☞ Add sliced almonds to a can of creamy onion sauce; pour over hot cooked cauliflower; sprinkle with grated cheese and place under the broiler for 5 minutes.

STRING BEAN CASSEROLE OR GREEN BEANS WITH BLACK WALNUTS

Serves 6

---

4 tablespoons butter	¼ pound American
6 tablespoons flour	cheese, diced
½ small bay leaf	3 cups cooked green
2 cups chicken stock	beans
	¼ cup chopped walnuts

☞ Brown butter in saucepan over low heat. Add flour and bay leaf. Stir until well blended. Remove from heat. Gradually add stock and return to heat. Cook, stirring constantly, until mixture is smooth and thickened. Add cheese and stir until melted. Arrange beans in casserole. Pour sauce over beans and sprinkle with chopped walnuts. Bake 20 minutes in moderate oven.

SWEET AND EASY CORN PUDDING

Serves about 8

---

2 cups corn (frozen,	2 eggs
canned or fresh)	¾ teaspoon salt
1 tablespoon flour	¾ cup milk
3 tablespoons sugar	½ stick butter

☞ Place all ingredients in a blender, mix 10 seconds at high speed. Pour into well-greased baking dish, dot with butter and bake 45 minutes at 375°.

CORN FRITTERS

Serves 6

---

2 cups corn, fresh or
canned
1 teaspoon salt
⅛ teaspoon pepper
1 egg, well beaten

1 teaspoon melted butter
½ cup milk
2 cups flour
1 teaspoon baking powder
fat for frying

☞ Chop corn very fine and add salt, pepper, egg, butter, milk, flour and baking powder. Mix well. Fry in hot deep fat, 1 tablespoon batter for each fritter. Serve with strips of fried bacon, or with brandy sauce (page 73).

HOMINY AU GRATIN

Serves 8

3½ cups (#2½ can)
hominy
1 cup water
1½ teaspoons salt
2 tablespoons finely
chopped green pepper

3 tablespoons grated
sharp cheese
3 tablespoons butter
1 cup milk

☞ Place hominy in heavy frying pan. Add water, salt, green pepper, cheese and butter. Cover and simmer over medium heat for 10 minutes. Add milk, stir well, and cook for 15 minutes over low heat, stirring occasionally. Serve hot.

FRIED CUCUMBERS

☞ Wash and slice cucumbers. Dip in beaten egg. Roll in flour and fry in butter until crispy brown.

ONIONS SUPREME

Serves 8 to 10

---

3 *large onions*	3 *eggs*
1 *stick of butter*	1 *lemon*
1 *tablespoon flour,*	1 *cup bread crumbs*
rounded	*paprika*
½ *cup milk*	

☞ Quarter 3 large onions, cook in salt water until tender. Drain and chop fine.

Melt ½ stick of butter in saucepan, blend in 1 rounded tablespoon of flour, add ½ cup of milk and 3 well beaten eggs. Stir in juice of 1 lemon.

Add onions to sauce and turn into buttered casserole. Cover with coarse bread crumbs. Sprinkle paprika over top. Pour ½ stick of melted butter over top. Brown in 400° oven until golden.

SWEET POTATO BALLS

Serves about 8

---

2 cups cooked fresh or
canned sweet potatoes
¼ stick of butter, melted
⅛ teaspoon salt
2 tablespoons granu-
lated sugar

⅛ teaspoon cinnamon
¼ teaspoon vanilla
marshmallows
crushed corn flakes
fat for frying

☞ Mash potatoes and add ingredients as listed, except marshmallows, cornflakes and fat. Mix well and form into balls around marshmallows, roll in cornflake crumbs and fry in deep fat or oil until brown.

CANDIED SWEET POTATOES

Serves 6

½ cup white sugar
⅓ cup brown sugar,
packed
⅔ cup water
pinch salt

3 tablespoons butter
½ teaspoon cinnamon
6 medium sweet pota-
toes

☞ Combine above ingredients (except potatoes) in pan and bring to hard boil, stirring well. Pour over drained cooked sweet potatoes in shallow pan and simmer until syrup has been absorbed. Serve piping hot.

CREAMED POTATOES AU GRATIN

Serves 6 to 8

---

4 cups diced uncooked potatoes	1 tablespoon chopped parsley
1½ teaspoons salt	2 tablespoons flour
2 cups milk	1 cup cold water
¼ cup grated sharp cheddar cheese	½ stick butter

☞ Place potatoes in saucepan and cover with water. Add 1 teaspoonful of the salt and boil over medium heat for approximately 10 minutes. Pour off the water and add to the cooked potatoes the remaining ½ teaspoonful of salt, milk, cheese, parsley, flour which has been dissolved in the cup of cold water, and the butter. Stir well and cook for approximately ten minutes more or until the potatoes are tender and the sauce is creamy and thick. Serve hot.

CREAMED MUSHROOMS

Serves 6 to 8

---

1 pound mushrooms	1½ tablespoons flour
5 teaspoons butter	½ cup thin cream
½ teaspoon salt	toast
few grains of pepper	

☞ Clean mushrooms, remove caps and cut both stems and caps in thin slices. Melt butter, add mushrooms and cook for 3 minutes in heavy saucepan. Sprinkle with salt and pepper, dredge with flour and pour the cream over. Cook 5 minutes, stirring constantly. Serve on toast.

BAKED STUFFED MUSHROOMS

Serves 6 to 8

1 pound mushrooms (about 12 medium-sized mushrooms)	¼ cup soft butter
	1 clove garlic, crushed
	¼ teaspoon thyme
1 cup finely chopped pecans	½ teaspoon salt
	½ cup heavy cream
3 tablespoons chopped parsley (or flakes)	

☞ Remove stems from mushrooms, wipe with damp cloth and arrange caps in baking dish bottom side up. Chop stems and mix with all ingredients except cream. Stuff mushrooms, pour cream over, cover and bake at 350° 30 to 45 minutes, or until tender. Baste occasionally.

SWEET-POTATO AND APPLE SCALLOP
Serves 6 to 8

---

2 cups cooked sweet
   potatoes, sliced
2 cups thinly sliced
   cooking apples

¾ cup fine dry bread
   crumbs
1 cup maple syrup
¼ cup butter, chopped nuts

☞ Arrange sweet potatoes, apples and crumbs in alternate layers in buttered baking dish. Add syrup, dot with butter, sprinkle with nuts and bake, covered, in hot oven (over 400°) until apples are tender.

DELICIOUS RICE
WITH MUSHROOMS
Serves 4 to 6

---

1 stick butter
1 medium-sized onion
1 cup long-grain un-
   cooked rice

4 chicken bouillon cubes
2 cups hot water
1 medium-sized can
   mushrooms

☞ Melt butter in medium-sized saucepan. Add chopped onion and rice and mix well. Cook over low heat until onion is transparent and rice is yellow. Dissolve bouillon cubes in hot water, and add to rice and onion mixture. Stir until well mixed, place cover on pan, and simmer for 1 hour. Just before rice is done, stir in drained mushrooms.

SPINACH RING WITH CHESTNUTS

Serves 12

---

4 *boxes frozen spinach*	*nutmeg*
1 *cup thick white sauce*	2 *cups chestnuts*
(*see page 69*)	1 *tablespoon cornstarch*
salt and pepper	

☞ Cook frozen spinach as directed. Drain. Stir in white sauce. Season with salt, pepper and a little nutmeg. Pack in buttered ring mold. Place in pan of water and bake about ½ hour in 350° oven. When ready to serve, unmold on hot platter and fill center with either chestnuts or mushrooms.

To prepare chestnuts:

Pierce skins of chestnuts with sharp knife. Place on pan in hot oven until inner and outer skins pop; remove skins. Cook chestnuts in small amount of salted water until tender. Mix with 1 tablespoon cornstarch and ½ cup cold water cooked until thick, and fill center of spinach ring. (When chestnuts are out of season, use sautéed mushrooms in center of ring, or fill with little Harvard beets.)

SPINACH SOUFFLÉ

Serves 8 to 10

---

3 packages frozen chopped spinach

1 large package cream cheese

1 small onion, chopped

3 eggs

4 cups clear broth (beef or chicken)

☞ Prepare spinach as package describes, then drain very well. Mix all ingredients well. Place in baking-and-serving casserole dish and bake 15 minutes at 300°.

STUFFED ACORN SQUASH

Serves 6

---

3 acorn squash

2 cups canned applesauce

⅓ cup brown sugar, packed

1 tablespoon lemon juice

⅓ cup seedless raisins

¼ cup broken walnut meats

2 tablespoons butter

☞ Scrub squash; halve lengthwise; remove seeds and stringy portions. Combine applesauce, sugar, lemon juice, raisins and nut meats; place in squash halves. Dot with butter. Place squash in baking dish; add enough hot water to cover bottom of dish. Cover; bake in hot oven (450°) 45 to 60 minutes, or until tender, removing cover after 20 to 30 minutes to brown.

STUFFED TOMATOES
Serves 6

---

6 *large smooth tomatoes*   *few drops onion juice*
salt and pepper   *1 cup fine bread crumbs,*
1 cup bread or cracker   *buttered*
crumbs

☞ Remove slice from stem end of each tomato. Take out
the seeds and pulp, leaving enough meat of the tomato to
form good shells. Sprinkle each one inside with salt and pepper and place upside down on rack to drain out the juice.
Chop the tomato pulp, add enough bread or cracker crumbs
to make proper consistency (as in stuffing). Season with salt,
pepper and onion juice. Then fill tomato shells, set them in a
baking pan and sprinkle with the buttered bread crumbs. Bake
in hot oven until brown.

BREADS

ROLLS

BISCUITS

BANANA BREAD

Makes medium loaf

½ cup Crisco	1 tablespoon sour milk
1 cup sugar	1 teaspoon soda
2 eggs	2 bananas
2 cups flour	½ cup nuts (optional)

☞ Cream Crisco, sugar and eggs. Add flour, milk, soda, crushed bananas, and nuts if used. Bake 1 hour at 350° in bread pan. Cool, slice and serve.

DELICIOUS SPOON BREAD

Serves 6 to 8

---

1 stick butter	3 cups boiling water
2 cups white corn meal	

Add butter to boiling water and gradually stir in corn meal. Cool. Add to this mixture:

5 tablespoons sugar	3 well-beaten eggs
1 teaspoon salt	1½ cups milk

Mix well, pour into buttered casserole baking dish. Bake 1 hour at 350°. Serve hot.

NUT RAISIN BREAD

Makes medium loaf

---

3 cups flour	1 cup English walnuts,
1 cup sugar	coarsely chopped
3 teaspoons baking	1 cup raisins
powder	1 cup milk
1 teaspoon salt	1 egg

☞ Combine dry ingredients. Add nuts and raisins that have been dredged well in flour. Combine milk and egg. Add to dry ingredients and mix well. Pour into loaf pan that has been greased and floured. Bake at 350° for about 1 hour. Slice to desired thickness.

ROLLS

Makes about 3 dozen rolls

½ cup sugar	2 cakes yeast
½ cup lard	¼ cup lukewarm water
2 cups boiling water	1 egg
dash salt	5 or 6 cups flour

☞ Combine first 4 ingredients. After well mixed, let come to room temperature. Soften yeast in ¼ cup lukewarm water. Add to first mixture. Beat egg and add. Sift in cups of flour, one at a time, until right consistency has been reached. Turn out on floured board and knead. Place in greased bowl. Let rise in warm place until double in bulk. Shape into rolls 2 hours before baking. Bake in 450° oven, 8 to 10 minutes.

REFRIGERATOR ROLLS

Makes about 3 dozen

---

1 cup boiling water	2 eggs, beaten
1 cup shortening	1 cake yeast
½ cup sugar	1 cup lukewarm water
1½ teaspoons salt	6 cups unsifted flour

☞ Pour 1 cup boiling water over shortening, sugar and salt. Blend and cool. Add beaten eggs. Let yeast stand in 1 cup lukewarm water 5 minutes, then stir and add to mixture.

Add flour. Blend well. Cover with oiled silk cover and place in refrigerator at least 4 hours.

About 3 hours before using rolls, roll into desired shapes, using enough extra flour to make them easy to handle, then place in greased pans and allow them to rise 3 hours until they are double their original size. Bake at 425° for 12-15 minutes. If harder crust is desired, bake at 350-375° for 20 minutes. If slick crust is wanted, rub with milk or egg white before baking, or with butter after.

SWEET-POTATO YEAST ROLLS

Makes 3 dozen rolls

1 cup sweet potatoes, mashed	1 cake yeast, dissolved in a little warm water
1 cup milk, scalded	2 eggs, beaten
1 stick butter	6 or 7 cups flour (enough
½ cup sugar	to make a soft dough)

☞ Mix potato, salt and milk together. Cream butter and sugar, then add the potato mixture, then the dissolved yeast cake and add to beaten eggs. Beat very thoroughly. Then add flour, 1 cup at a time, enough to make a soft dough. Let stand to rise in a warm place (about 80°). Punch down in the pan after the dough rises for 1 hour, then shape into rolls and let rise again for 1 hour. Then bake at 450° for about 20 minutes until nicely browned. Do not overcook. Rolls should be very light and soft.

DINNER ROLLS

Makes 24 rolls

---

2 cups milk	2 yeast cakes
3 tablespoons butter	½ cup lukewarm water
3 teaspoons salt	2 eggs
½ cup sugar	4 cups flour

☞ Heat first 4 ingredients to lukewarm. Add yeast softened in water. Beat eggs well and add mixture. Beat mixture thoroughly, then sift in the 4 cups flour and beat well. Knead in more flour to make it workable, but keep the dough soft. Place dough in bowl, cover with cloth, place where warm. Let rise to top of bowl, press dough down, then shape rolls and place close together in lightly buttered baking pan. Let rise above pan. Bake in 350° oven until brown.

CHEESE BISCUITS

Makes 3 dozen

---

1 pound Old English cheese	1 pound of flour (4 cups)
½ pound butter or margarine	1 teaspoon salt
	¼ teaspoon red pepper

☞ Let butter and cheese come to room temperature. Combine and mix together. Add other ingredients. Roll on floured board and cut into biscuits. Place on greased cookie sheet and bake in hot oven (400°). These biscuits can be made ahead of time and kept in the refrigerator until needed.

CREAM BISCUITS

Makes about 2 dozen

---

4 cups flour
¼ stick butter
1 teaspoon salt
3 teaspoons cream of
tartar

1½ teaspoons baking
soda
2 cups rich sweet
cream

☞ Mix above ingredients together. The dough should be very soft. Roll thin, cut with biscuit cutter and bake in hot oven (400°) about 15 minutes.

MARYLAND BEATEN BISCUITS

(OLD EASTERN SHORE RECIPE)
Makes 6 dozen

---

2 pounds flour
6 ounces lard
scant teaspoon salt
½ teaspoon sugar

1 cup cold water
pinch baking soda size
of pea (no larger)

☞ Work all ingredients together well, have dough stiff. Beat 20 minutes with iron mallet. To shape biscuits, squeeze dough through hole made by thumb and forefinger, pinch off and pat down a little. Place on baking sheet and prick 3 times with fork. Bake in oven about 400° for 25 minutes.

PECAN MUFFINS

Makes 12 large or 24 small muffins

---

1 cup whole-wheat flour	¾ teaspoon salt
4 tablespoons brown sugar	½ cup chopped pecans
4 teaspoons baking powder	1 cup milk
1 cup flour	1 egg
	4 tablespoons shortening, melted

☞ Mix together dry ingredients. Add nuts, milk, egg, melted shortening, and beat well. Put 1 tablespoon batter in each greased muffin-pan section and bake in hot oven (425°) 18 to 25 minutes, depending on size of muffin.

BLUEBERRY GINGERBREAD

Serves 10 to 12

1½ cups fresh blueberries (dry)	1 cup molasses
½ cup butter	2½ cups sifted flour
½ cup sugar	1 teaspoon baking soda
2 eggs, unbeaten	1 teaspoon ground ginger
1 cup buttermilk	

☞ Cream butter and sugar. Add eggs, buttermilk and molasses. Sift dry ingredients and add to mixture. Do not over-beat. Fold in blueberries. Pour into nine-inch ring mold (greased and floured). Bake at 350° for 40 minutes. Serve hot or cold with nutmeg-flavored whipped cream.

BREAD STICKS

Makes about 3 dozen

1 *cup milk, scalded*	3¾ *cups flour, sifted into*
1 *tablespoon sugar*	*large bowl*
1 *teaspoon salt*	3 *eggs, separated*
½ *stick butter*	*(yolks used for*
1 *cake yeast or 1 pack-*	*brushing tops)*
age dry yeast	

☞ Scald milk. Add sugar, salt and butter. Stir until butter is melted. Take 4 tablespoonfuls of this and dissolve yeast in it. Add to flour. Beat egg whites until stiff and add to mixture. Mix well. Knead in bowl for 1 minute. Cover. Let rise until double in bulk. Turn out on well-floured pastry cloth, cut into pieces and roll out about 6 or 7 inches long—the thickness of a finger. Place ¼ inch apart on greased cookie sheet. Brush with beaten egg yolks mixed with 1 tablespoon water. Sprinkle with crystal salt, poppy seeds, caraway, or anything desired. Let rise ½ hour and bake in 400° oven, 35 to 40 minutes. These will be very crisp (can be frozen).

CHEESE STRAWS

Makes 3 dozen

½ cup corn meal	½ cup Parmesan cheese,
1 cup flour, sifted	grated
1 teaspoon salt	¼ cup milk
⅓ cup shortening	paprika

☞ Sift together corn meal, flour and salt. Cut in shortening as for pastry. Stir in cheese and milk. Knead gently on a lightly floured board. Roll to ⅛-inch thickness, cut into long strips with pastry cutter and sprinkle with paprika. Bake on cookie sheets in 400° oven 8 to 10 minutes. Cheese straws are especially good with a crisp salad.

HOT CAKES

---

2 cups sifted flour	2 cups buttermilk or
1 teaspoon baking soda	sour milk
½ teaspoon salt	1½ tablespoons melted
1 tablespoon sugar	margarine or other
1 egg, beaten thoroughly	shortening

☞ For really good hot cakes, mix flour, baking soda, salt and sugar. After you think they are well mixed, sift all the ingredients again. Mix thoroughly beaten egg with buttermilk or sour milk. Add this to the dry ingredients gradually and beat until smooth. Add melted margarine or shortening. Let the batter sit for a while in the refrigerator and then try your luck with the griddle.

Comments

1. The recipe as given above is just right as is, if you like your hot cakes medium thick. However, I like thin hot cakes, so I use about 2½ cups of buttermilk to 2 cups flour. One finds by trial the favorite consistency for one's personal taste, so that the cakes are thin but brown nicely. They should not be made so thin that the batter is watery and runs out to a ragged lace edge on the griddle.

2. A great deal of the eye-appeal in cooking perfect hot cakes comes from having the griddle just right as regards to temperature. It should not be too hot, but hot enough. If you use gas for cooking, the gas flame should not be turned up full blast as that burns the hot cakes. If the griddle is not hot enough the hot cakes finish up a sickly, unattractive pale gray. The gas flame should be turned up about halfway so that the flame is about an inch high.

3. I have found that a thick, heavy, old-fashioned frying pan or "skillet" makes better hot cakes than any of the new-fangled thin aluminum griddles.

4. A hot cake should be baked, not fried. Of course, the griddle must be greased ever so lightly to keep the hot cakes from burning. A bacon rind is the best thing for the job, although any fat will do. But there should be just enough grease to turn the trick and not a particle more. Don't let the griddle get too hot. It is hot griddles that make cooks pour on too much shortening. When the cake is cooked on a griddle not too hot, but hot enough, it will be a deep golden reddish-brown that makes one hungry to look at it.

5. Cakes are not at their best if the batter is made up just before the hot cakes are to be cooked. I make up my batter the evening before and cook the hot cakes the first thing next morning after the batter has sat all night in the

refrigerator. I keep the batter in the refrigerator for several days and use the same pitcher or bowl of hot cake batter for several days until I have used it all up. It seems to get better each day.

FRENCH TOAST WITH PINEAPPLE

Serves 4

---

4 eggs	1 cup pineapple juice
1 teaspoon salt	8 slices bread
¾ teaspoon cinnamon	butter or margarine
3 tablespoons sugar	16 slices bacon

☞ Beat eggs until light. Add salt, cinnamon, sugar and pineapple juice. Beat well. Dip slices of bread in this mixture and fry gently in butter or margarine until golden brown. Serve with crisp bacon.

WAFFLES

(EASY AND GOOD) *Serves 4*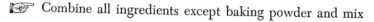

1½ cups sifted flour	1¼ cups milk
½ teaspoon salt	4 tablespoons melted
3 heaping tablespoons	butter
sugar	3 teaspoons baking
1 egg	powder

☞ Combine all ingredients except baking powder and mix

well. Fold in baking powder just before cooking. Cook in waffle iron and serve at once.

OLD-FASHIONED DOUGHNUTS

Makes about 1½ dozen

---

2 *cups sifted flour*	1 *egg*
½ *teaspoon baking soda*	½ *teaspoon vanilla*
⅛ *teaspoon nutmeg*	2 *tablespoons vinegar*
¼ *teaspoon salt*	*plus enough milk to*
2 *tablespoons shortening*	*make ½ cup*
½ *cup sugar*	*fat for frying*

☞ Sift flour, baking soda, nutmeg and salt together. Cream shortening, add sugar gradually, continue creaming. Add egg; beat well. Add vanilla. Add combined vinegar and milk alternately with dry ingredients. Stir only until well blended. Roll small quantities of the dough at a time, about ⅓ inch thick. Cut doughnuts and let stand about 10 minutes. Fry on each side in hot fat (365°) to a delicate brown.

OLD-FASHIONED DUMPLINGS

Serves about 8

---

1 *cup flour*	½ *teaspoon salt*
2 *teaspoons yeast powder*	1 *egg*

☞ Mix ingredients together and add enough water to make a sticky dough. Drop into gravy and cook 10 minutes. Do not remove cover on pan until ready to take dumplings out.

CANDIES AND PUDDINGS

DIVINITY CANDY

Makes 24 to 30 pieces

---

2 cups sugar	whites of two eggs
¼ cup water	1 teaspoon vanilla
½ cup light corn syrup	1 cup chopped nuts

☞ Boil sugar, water and syrup together until it will form a soft ball. Let cool a little, then pour slowly on beaten egg whites, stirring constantly. Add vanilla and nuts. Drop by teaspoonfuls on buttered pan and cool.

FUDGE

---

2 cups sugar
1 cup milk
3 squares unsweetened
  chocolate

pinch salt
lump butter
1 teaspoon vanilla

☞ Combine 2 cups sugar and 1 cup milk in saucepan. Heat, do not boil. Add 3 squares of unsweetened chocolate and pinch of salt. Boil until soft ball forms when dropped in cold water. Remove from heat. Add a good-sized lump of butter and 1 teaspoon vanilla. Beat until mixture loses gloss and thickens. Pour into buttered pan. Cool until firm. Cut in squares.

PEANUT BUTTER
FUDGE

Makes 18 to 20 pieces

---

2 cups sugar
3 tablespoons cocoa
½ cup cream

1 teaspoon vanilla
½ pound (1 cup) peanut
  butter

☞ Combine sugar and cocoa. Mix well. Add cream and bring to boil for 3 minutes. Remove from heat, add vanilla and peanut butter. Beat until stiff and drop 1 teaspoonful at a time on greased pan. Cool.

PEANUT BRITTLE

(EXCEPTIONALLY GOOD)

Makes 20 pieces

2 cups sugar	1 cup or more raw pea-
½ cup warm water	nuts
⅔ cup light corn syrup	2 teaspoon baking soda

☞ Boil sugar, water and syrup until it spins a hair, then add the raw peanuts. Cook slowly until syrup becomes light yellow. Peanuts will brown during this period. Add soda, and when mixture foams up, take off stove and pour out on a porcelain-top table that has been well buttered. Let cool. When cool enough to handle, take a wooden mallet and break up into pieces. Keeps indefinitely in air-tight can.

CHOCOLATE NUT CRUNCH DESSERT

Serves 9 to 10

2 cups vanilla wafer crumbs	1½ squares unsweetened chocolate, melted
1 cup chopped walnuts	½ teaspoon vanilla
½ cup butter	3 egg whites, stiffly beaten
1 cup powdered sugar	
3 egg yolks, well beaten	

☞ Combine crumbs and nuts. Line 9-inch square pan with half of crumb mix. Cream butter and sugar, add egg yolks, chocolate and vanilla. Fold in stiffly beaten egg whites. Spread over crumb mix in pan. Top with remaining crumb mix. Chill in refrigerator overnight. Cut into squares and top with whipped cream.

SPICED PECANS

2 cups pecan halves	5 tablespoons water
1 cup sugar	2 teaspoons vanilla
1 teaspoon cinnamon	

☞ Warm nuts in 275° oven for 8 minutes. Boil sugar, cinnamon and water to soft-ball stage. Remove from heat and add vanilla. Beat slightly and add pecans. Stir to coat well each pecan half. Turn on to buttered cookie sheet and separate, using two forks. Serve when cool.

TRIFLE
Serves 8 to 10

☞ Line a bowl with sponge cake (page 138). Make boiled custard:

1 quart milk	1½ cups sugar
5 egg yolks	1 teaspoon vanilla

☞ Cook all ingredients together until thick, stirring constantly. When cool, pour over cake, top with lots of whipped cream and serve.

CHARLOTTE RUSSE

Serves 12

---

2 envelopes unflavored gelatin	1 teaspoon vanilla extract
½ cup cold water	1½ dozen ladyfingers, split
2 cups milk	
6 eggs, separated	2 cups heavy cream, whipped
1 cup sugar	

☞ Soften gelatin in water. Scald milk in top of double boiler. Beat egg yolks and sugar until well blended; stir into milk. Cook over boiling water, stirring constantly, until mixture coats a spoon (about 5 minutes). Remove from heat. Add gelatin; stir until dissolved. Add vanilla. Cool thoroughly. Meanwhile line sides of 10" by 4" tube pan with ladyfingers. When custard is cool, beat egg whites until stiff, fold into custard. Fold in cream. Turn into pan. Chill until set.

BREAD PUDDING

Serves 6 to 8

---

4 eggs	1 quart milk
1 cup sugar	½ teaspoon salt
2 tablespoons butter	1 cup raisins
1 cup bread crumbs	nutmeg

☞ Beat eggs, sugar and butter together, then add bread crumbs, milk and salt. Put in glass casserole and just before placing in oven, add raisins and grated nutmeg on top. Bake for 1 hour, or until set, at 325°. Serve with brandy sauce (page 73).

OLD-FASHIONED BOILED OR BAG PUDDING

(SLICES LIKE CAKE)

Serves 6 to 8

3 eggs, beaten light	a little orange peel
2 cups sugar	1/4 pound citron
1/2 teaspoon salt	1/4 pound beef suet, ground
1/2 teaspoon nutmeg	1 cup water or milk
1 cup raisins and 1 cup currants, boiled 5 minutes	2 teaspoons yeast powder
	3 cups flour

☞ Mix all together, shape into a round loaf and put into a twill cotton bag. Tie one end and drop bag into boiling water to cover. Boil 2 hours.

Sauce:

1 cup milk	2 teaspoons cornstarch mixed in a little water
1 egg, beaten light	
sugar to taste (about 1 cup)	pinch salt
	2 tablespoons wine, or 1/2 teaspoon vanilla
butter size of walnut	

☞ Bring milk to boil and add remaining ingredients. Boil together until creamy. Serve over pudding.

LEMON FLUFF

Serves 12

1¾ cups evaporated milk	¼ cup lemon juice
1 package (3 ounces)	1 cup sugar
lemon-flavor gelatin	2½ cups vanilla wafer
1¾ cups hot water	crumbs

☞ Chill unopened can of milk in refrigerator until icy cold, about 3 or 4 hours. Dissolve gelatin in hot water. Chill until partly set. Whip until light and fluffy. Add lemon juice and sugar. Whip chilled milk and fold into gelatin mixture. Line bottom of 9″ by 13″ pan with crumbs. Pour in gelatin mixture, sprinkle with remaining crumbs. Chill until firm. Cut in squares and center each with maraschino cherry.

OLD ENGLISH PLUM PUDDING

(A R E C I P E U S E D I N M A R Y L A N D F O R 7 5 Y E A R S)

Serves 8 to 10

2 cups beef suet	½ pound seedless
1 egg	raisins
2 cups flour	1½ teaspoons cinnamon
1 cup brown sugar,	½ teaspoon nutmeg
packed	enough milk to mois-
1 teaspoon baking powder	ten above ingredients
1 teaspoon salt	

☞ Cut the suet into small pieces. Add all of above ingredients as listed. Then mix with just enough milk to hold mixture together in a sticky consistency. Place in a heavy greased piece of muslin and sprinkle with flour. Tie up like a bag. Then steam in a pudding steamer for 2 hours. Remove from bag, slice and serve with brandy sauce (page 73).

MOLDED STRAWBERRY
CHIFFON DESSERT

Serves 8 to 10

1 pint strawberries	½ cup milk
⅔ cup sugar	½ teaspoon vanilla
1 envelope unflavored	2 egg whites
gelatin	1 cup heavy whipping
⅛ teaspoon salt	cream

☞ Wash and hull strawberries, mash berries, sprinkle with 2 tablespoons of sugar and set aside. Reserve 4 tablespoons of the sugar to beat with egg whites. Mix together remaining sugar, gelatin and salt in saucepan, stir in milk. Place over low heat and cook, stirring constantly, until gelatin is dissolved. Remove from heat. Add mashed strawberries. Chill, stirring occasionally, until mixture mounds slightly when dropped from a spoon. Beat egg whites until stiff, but not dry. Gradually add reserved 4 tablespoons sugar and beat until very stiff. Fold into gelatin mixture. Fold in whipped cream. Turn into a 6-cup ring mold. Chill until firm. Unmold and fill center with additional strawberries and whipped cream.

SPANISH CREAM

Serves 10 to 12

---

2 envelopes unflavored
gelatin
3 cups milk
3 eggs, yolks and whites
beaten separately

1 cup sugar
pinch salt
1 teaspoon vanilla

☞ Dissolve gelatin in milk over medium heat and let it come to a boil. Cream egg yolks and sugar well and then add to the hot milk mixture and boil until it thickens like a custard. Add salt, then stir in the well-beaten egg whites and vanilla. Pour into custard cups or sherbet glasses. Chill and serve with whipped cream, if desired.

STRAWBERRY CREAM

À LA MARYLAND

Serves 8

---

2 quarts fresh straw-
berries
4 tablespoons sugar

1 pint whipping cream
¾ cup plain cream
4 tablespoons port wine

☞ Wash strawberries and remove caps. Place 1½ quarts of the strawberries, in equal portions, in 8 glass dessert dishes. Mash the remainder of the berries in a large wire strainer, and add the sugar to the juice obtained from the berries. Whip pint of whipping cream until stiff. Fold sweetened juice into the whipped cream, and then add the plain cream. Fold in the port wine. Pour whipped cream mixture over whole strawberries in dessert glasses. Chill. To decorate, if desired, top with whipped cream and a whole strawberry before serving.

BAVARIAN CREAM

Serves 10 to 12

1 envelope unflavored gelatin	1 cup crushed pineapple (drained)
1 cup cold water	½ cup maraschino cherries (cut up)
1 pint milk	
1 cup sugar	½ cup chopped nuts (pecans or walnuts)
pinch salt	1 pint whipping cream

☞ Soak gelatin for 15 minutes in cup of cold water. Heat ½ pint of milk, not boiling, and stir into gelatin. Mix remainder of cold milk with sugar and salt. Add to gelatin mixture. Let stiffen, then add pineapple, cherries and nuts. Carefully fold in stiffly whipped cream. Refrigerate in sherbert glasses three hours before serving. Add spoonful of whipped cream on top if desired.

PEPPERMINT ICE CREAM

Serves 8

☞ Melt 16 marshmallows with 1 cup milk. Chill until thick and syrupy. Add 1 cup heavy cream. Add a few drops of red food coloring, then ¾ cup of crushed peppermint candy. Freeze in ice trays.

CRÊPES SUZETTE
Serves 12

---

2 *tablespoons sugar*	1 *quart milk*
6 *eggs, beaten*	2 *cups sifted flour*
6 *tablespoons melted butter, not hot*	

☞ Stir sugar into beaten eggs. Add butter, milk and flour. Have 5-inch iron frying pan hot and use a teaspoon of batter for each pancake.

Pour a small amount of batter in the pan and tilt it back and forth so the batter will spread and cover the whole frying pan. When brown, turn and brown on the other side.

Stack pancakes until ready to be served with Suzette sauce (page 70) or brandy sauce (page 73).

HOLIDAY FLAMING
SUNDAE
Serves 6

½ *cup sugar*	¼ *cup chopped nuts*
½ *cup water*	1 *quart vanilla ice cream*
¼ *cup chopped maraschino cherries*	6 *sugar cubes*
1 *cup prepared mincemeat*	*lemon extract*

☞ Combine sugar and water and boil for 5 minutes. Remove from heat and add cherries, mincemeat and nuts. Cool. Divide ice cream into 6 servings. Spoon sauce over ice cream. Just before serving, dip sugar cube into lemon extract, push down slightly on very top of ice cream and ignite. Serve flaming.

CRÈME DE MENTHE ICE CREAM PARFAIT

Serves 8

1 quart French vanilla ice cream	1 jar of green maraschino cherries
16 tablespoons crème de menthe	½ pint heavy cream, whipped

☞ Reserve eight of the cherries for decoration and chop remaining cherries into small pieces. Place one tablespoonful of crème de menthe in bottom of each of eight parfait glasses. Add one dip of ice cream to each glass and then add one-eighth portion of the chopped cherries to each. Add another dip of ice cream and pour one more tablespoonful of crème de menthe over top of ice cream. Top parfait with one tablespoonful of whipped cream and decorate with a green cherry.

CARAMEL CUSTARD

Serves 6

---

4 *eggs*	1 *cup sugar*
3 *cups milk*	1 *teaspoon vanilla*
¼ *teaspoon salt*	¼ *teaspoon nutmeg*

☞ Beat eggs for one minute with rotary egg beater. Add sugar and salt to eggs and beat again until well mixed. Beat in milk, nutmeg, and vanilla. Pour into custard cups that have been rinsed with cold water. Set cups into a shallow pan containing ½ inch of hot water. Bake in 350° oven 20 to 30 minutes, or until custard is firm. Do not overcook. Cool. When ready to serve, loosen custard by running a knife around inside of cup and turn upside down on dessert dish. Pour caramel sauce over each custard, and decorate with sprig of mint.

CARAMEL SAUCE

Makes about 2 cups

---

1 *cup sugar*   ½ *cup boiling water*   2 *tablespoons cream*

☞ Place sugar in heavy pan and heat slowly until melted and browned, stirring constantly. Add boiling water slowly, stirring vigorously. Cook until sirupy and until all of the browned sugar is melted. Remove from heat and add cream. Serve hot or cold. If too thick when cold, add a little more cream.

SNOW PUDDING
Serves 8

---

2 envelopes unflavored
gelatin
1 cup cold water
1 cup boiling water

1 cup sugar
juice of 2 lemons
2 egg whites, well beaten

☞ Soak gelatin in cold water 5 minutes, then add boiling water, sugar, and lemon juice. Strain and then let stand until it begins to set. Add beaten egg whites and beat until fluffy. Pile in sherbet glasses and chill before serving.

EASTERN SHORE DATE PUDDING

(FOR THOSE WHO WANT A RICH-SEEMING DESSERT THAT ISN'T !)

Serves 6

---

4 eggs
2 cups chopped dates
2 cups chopped pecans
1½ cups sugar

4 level tablespoons flour
2 teaspoons baking pow-
der
2 teaspoons vanilla

☞ Beat eggs slightly. Add all other ingredients. Stir. Bake in well-greased dish 40 minutes in 375° oven. Slice and serve with plenty of cream, if desired. Delicious cold or reheated after several days in refrigerator.

STRAWBERRY FLUFF

Serves 6 to 8

1 egg white	½ cup crushed strawber-
lemon juice	ries, undrained
½ cup sugar	whipping cream or
	plain cream

☞ Beat egg white slightly, adding a few drops of lemon juice. Gradually whip in the sugar and crushed berries, alternately. Whip until mixture expands to fill a quart bowl and is exceedingly light and fluffy. Pile into tall, slender glasses or sherbet cups. Chill thoroughly. Serve with whipped cream or plain cream. For a richer dessert, fold in 1 cup whipped cream after mixture has been thoroughly chilled. Garnish with strawberries.

PEACH FLUFF

Serves 6 to 8

Peach Fluff is a favorite dessert because it is light and airy, yet full of wonderful peach flavor. It can be made the day before needed or in the cool of the morning.

1 can (1 pound) cling peaches	1 package (3 ounce) or-
½ cup whipping cream	ange-flavor gelatin

☞ Thoroughly drain peaches, reserving syrup. Crush

peaches to make about 1½ cups pulp. Measure syrup and add water, if necessary, to make 1 cup liquid. Heat and dissolve gelatin in it. Blend in peach pulp. Cook until slightly thickened. Whip cream until stiff and fold into gelatin. Turn into 1 quart mold or individual molds and chill until firm.

PIES

PASTRY FOR PIE

1 cup sifted flour
3 teaspoons sugar
⅛ teaspoon salt

1 teaspoon baking pow-
der
⅓ cup shortening
1 tablespoon cold water

Mix well, roll out on floured board and spread over a 9-inch pie plate. Crimp edges and bake in hot oven (375°) until light brown.

MERINGUE

4 egg whites
½ teaspoon cream of
tartar

1 cup sugar

☞ Beat egg whites until frothy, sift cream of tartar over the top and beat until stiff. Sprinkle 1 cup sugar, 2 tablespoons at a time, over the meringue. Beat until sugar disappears before adding more. Pour meringue into pie pan. Shape the meringue to the pan with a spoon. (Keep the meringue the same thickness all over if possible.) Bake in a slow oven, (275°) for 1 hour. Transfer to cake rack to cool.

VANILLA-WAFER PIE CRUST

1 box (7-14 ounces) vanilla wafers, crushed to make 2 cups fine crumbs	*½ cup melted butter or margarine* *¼ cup sugar*

☞ Combine fine crumbs, butter and sugar. Press to sides and bottom of heart-shaped pan or 10-inch pie pan. Chill thoroughly.

CRUMB PIE CRUST

¼ cup melted butter	*1½ cups (about 5 ounces) crushed vanilla wafers*

☞ Mix butter and wafers. Press evenly over inside of 9-inch pie pan. Bake at 375° for 15 minutes.

CRUNCH PIE

Serves 6

6 cups sliced fruit (apples or fresh peaches)	1 teaspoon baking powder
1½ cups sugar	pinch of salt
1 cup flour	1 egg, beaten
	½ cup butter

☞ Fill baking dish with fruit that has been mixed with 1 cup sugar. Combine flour, ½ cup sugar, baking powder and salt. Add beaten egg to dry mixture. Mix until crumbly. Spread over fruit. Melt butter and spread over entire mixture. Bake 1 hour at 350°

CHOCOLATE NUT PIE

Serves 6

2 squares unsweetened chocolate	1 cup walnut meats vanilla-wafer cookie
1⅓ cup (1 can) sweetened condensed milk	crust (page 129)
½ cup hot water	½ cup heavy cream, whipped stiff

☞ Melt chocolate in top of boiler. Add sweetened condensed milk, and stir over boiling water 5 minutes, or until mixture thickens. Add water, stir until thoroughly blended. Add ½ cup chopped walnut meats. Pour into prepared crust, cover with whipped cream and sprinkle with remaining chopped nut meats. Chill thoroughly.

GLAZED STRAWBERRY
CREAM PIE

Serves 6

☞ Bake a single crust pie shell (page 128). While cooling make filling:

---

4 tablespoons corn- starch	3 egg yolks, slightly beaten
1 cup sugar	3 tablespoons butter
½ teaspoon salt	1 teaspoon vanilla
2 cups milk, scalded	

☞ Mix cornstarch, sugar and salt. Gradually add scalded milk. Cook in double boiler till thick, stirring constantly. Add small amount of mixture to beaten egg yolks; stir in remaining hot mixture. Remove from heat, add butter and vanilla and cool. When cool, pour into cooled baked pie crust. Arrange washed whole fresh strawberries on top of the custard.

Glaze:

1 cup boiling water	1 box strawberry flavor gelatin

☞ Pour boiling water over the gelatin. Let cool until it reaches a syrupy stage. Spoon over the strawberries and place pie in refrigerator until cool. Just before serving, decorate with sweetened whipped cream. This recipe can be made up into individual tarts if desired.

ANGEL PIE
Serves 6

4 egg whites	1 cup sugar
¼ teaspoon cream of	½ teaspoon vanilla
tartar	½ teaspoon almond fla-
¼ teaspoon salt	voring

☞ Beat egg whites to a froth. Add cream of tartar and salt. Add sugar, 1 teaspoon at a time, beating after each addition. Add flavorings. Spoon into well-buttered 9-inch pie plate and spread smoothly. Bake in 300° oven for 1 hour. Cool. (This will puff up and then fall.)

Fill with the following:

4 egg yolks	1½ cups whipping cream
½ cup sugar	grated rind of 1
4 tablespoons lemon juice	lemon

☞ Beat egg yolks until thick. Add sugar and lemon juice and rind. Cook 5 to 8 minutes in top of double boiler. Cool. Whip cream until stiff. Add half of it to custard, mixing well. Put in pie shell. Before serving, spread balance of whipped cream over pie.

GEORGE WASHINGTON
APPLE PIE
Serves 6

---

1 cup sugar	pastry (page 128)
1 cup unsweetened pine-apple juice (canned)	1 teaspoon cornstarch
	⅛ teaspoon salt
6 medium-sized tart apples	½ teaspoon vanilla
	1 tablespoon butter

☞ Boil sugar and pineapple juice. When mixture has boiled, add apples (pared, cored and cut into quarters). Cook slowly, uncovered, until fruit is tender, moving apples barely enough to keep them covered with the syrup. In this way fruit is kept whole. Lift apples carefully out with spoon and lay them in pie pan lined with pastry. Dissolve cornstarch in a little cold water (about 2 teaspoons) and add to syrup. Cook several minutes or until syrup thickens. Add salt, vanilla and butter and pour over apples. Cut strips of pastry (½-inch wide), brush lightly with cream or beaten egg mixed with water. Place strips criss-cross fashion over pie. Bake in hot oven (450°) for 10 minutes. Then reduce heat to 350° and bake approximately 35 minutes.

COCONUT PIE
Serves 6

3 eggs	1 medium-sized coconut,
1 cup sugar	grated
4 cups milk	1 teaspoon vanilla
½ stick butter	crumb crust (page 129)

Beat eggs and sugar together. Add milk, melted butter, coconut and vanilla. Combine ingredients thoroughly. Bake with pastry or crumb crust in medium oven. Test occasionally with silver knife. When filling does not adhere to knife, pie is done.

EASILY PREPARED FRESH PEACH PIE
Serves 6

1 package (3 ounces) peach or lemon flavor gelatin	2 peeled peaches, sliced very thin or diced
1¼ cups hot water	¼ cup sugar
1 pint vanilla or peach ice cream	1 baked pastry shell (page 128) or crumb crust (page 129)
	1 cup whipping cream

Put gelatin into 2-quart bowl. Add hot water, stir until dissolved. Add ice cream in four parts. Mix thoroughly after each part is added. Chill about 20 minutes. Mix peaches with sugar. Fold into gelatin mixture. Pour into pie shell. Chill at least 2 hours. Spread whipped cream over top of pie before cutting.

DELICIOUS PUMPKIN PIE

Serves 6

2 tablespoons flour	1 cup whole milk
¼ cup cold water	1 teaspoon vanilla
¼ cup boiling water	3 drops lemon extract
¼ pound butter	3 egg whites, beaten
1 cup pumpkin (fresh	nutmeg
or canned)	9-inch pie pan lined
3 egg yolks, beaten	with uncooked pie
¼ teaspoon salt	crust (page 128)
1 cup sugar	whipped cream
1 can evaporated milk	

☞ Mix flour and cold water to paste. Add boiling water and mix. Melt butter in saucepan and add pumpkin. Stir well into first mixture. To the above batter add egg yolks, salt, sugar, evaporated milk, whole milk, vanilla, and lemon extract. Fold in egg whites and small amount of nutmeg.

Pour into pie crust. Sprinkle few grains nutmeg on top. Bake 15 minutes in 400° oven. Reduce heat to 350° and bake 20 to 25 minutes longer. Top with whipped cream.

FROZEN LEMON PIE

Serves 8 to 10

---

3 egg yolks	2 tablespoons sugar
½ teaspoon salt	1 cup whipped cream
½ cup sugar	½ teaspoon vanilla
¼ cup lemon juice	1 cup vanilla wafers or
1 teaspoon vanilla	macaroon crumbs
3 egg whites, beaten stiff	

☞ Mix first 5 ingredients and cook in double boiler. Continue cooking until the mixture coats the spoon. Allow to cool. Fold into first mixture egg whites, sugar, whipped cream and vanilla.

Put half of wafer or macaroon crumbs in bottom of 9-inch square pan, pour in and spread mixture. Spread remaining crumbs on top. Place in freezer 24 hours or more before serving. Cut in squares and top with whipped cream if desired.

This is an excellent dessert to serve at the end of a large dinner.

LEMON ANGEL PIE

Serves 6

---

4 egg yolks	¼ cup water
½ cup sugar	1 cup cream, whipped
1 lemon, juice and	1 meringue shell (page
grated peel	128)

☞ Beat egg yolks until thick and light-colored. Add sugar, lemon juice, grated peel and water. Cook over water, stirring constantly until thick. Cool.

Spread half the whipped cream over the meringue shell. Top with lemon filling. Chill. Top with remaining whipped cream.

OLD-FASHIONED LEMON PIE

Serves 6

1¼ cups warm water	⅛ teaspoon salt
1 cup sugar	3 egg whites
juice 1 lemon (¼ cup)	3 tablespoons sugar
3 egg yolks	pie shell (page 128)
1 tablespoon butter	and meringue (page 128)
3 level tablespoons cornstarch	

☞ Mix all ingredients together in top of double boiler and cook until thick. Let cool and spread smoothly in prebaked pie shell. Top with meringue.

CAKES
ICINGS
COOKIES

SPONGE CAKE

Serves 10

---

6 egg yolks	1½ cups sugar
½ cup cold water	1½ cups flour
½ teaspoon vanilla	¼ teaspoon salt
½ teaspoon orange or lemon extract	6 egg whites
¼ teaspoon almond extract	¾ teaspoon cream of tartar

☞ Beat egg yolks until thick and lemon-colored. Add water and extracts and continue beating, gradually adding sugar, flour and salt, which have been mixed together.

Beat egg whites, add cream of tartar. Fold into first mixture. Pour into tube pan. Bake about 1 hour at 325° or until cake springs back to the touch.

QUICK COFFEE CAKE

1¼ cups flour	⅔ cup sugar
1½ teaspoons baking powder	3 tablespoons shortening
¼ teaspoon salt	5 tablespoons milk
	1 egg

☞ Sift dry ingredients. Cut in shortening. Add milk and egg. Spread in 9-inch square pan.

Topping:

3 tablespoons melted butter	½ teaspoon cinnamon
8 tablespoons flour	1 teaspoon vanilla
pinch salt	4 tablespoons confectioners' sugar

☞ Combine and sprinkle over batter. Bake in 350° oven for 25 to 30 minutes.

DELICIOUS APPLESAUCE CAKE

Makes a very large cake

---

1 cup margarine	3 teaspoons baking soda
2 cups sugar	2 teaspoons cinnamon
2 eggs	1 teaspoon ground cloves
2 16-ounce cans apple-	½ teaspoon salt
sauce	1 cup nuts
4 cups flour	2 cups raisins

 Cream margarine and sugar. Add eggs and applesauce. Mix well. Sift flour, soda, cinnamon, cloves and salt. Add to first mixture and beat well. Add nuts and raisins. Pour batter into greased and floured tube pan. Bake in 325° oven for 1¼ hours.

ORANGE CAKE

(MOST ECONOMICAL , BEST-STORING
AND MOST DELICIOUS CAKE RECIPE)

---

1 cup Crisco	¾ teaspoon salt
2 cups sugar	1 cup buttermilk
4 eggs	1 teaspoon lemon ex-
3 cups sifted flour	tract
½ teaspoon baking pow-	1 teaspoon orange ex-
der	tract
½ teaspoon baking soda	

 Cream Crisco, add sugar gradually and cream well. Add unbeaten eggs one at a time and beat well between each ad-

dition. (To this point, the longer the batter is beaten the smoother the texture of the cake.)

Add sifted dry ingredients a little at a time, alternating with buttermilk, beginning and ending with flour mixture. Beat just enough to blend after each addition. Add extracts.

Pour into heavy, well-greased and floured tube cake pan and bake 1 hour and 10 minutes at 325°.

As soon as removed from oven (leave in pan), spoon the following mixture over hot cake: ½ cup sugar mixed into ½ cup freshly squeezed orange juice.

APRICOT UPSIDE-DOWN CAKE

Serves 8 to 10

¼ cup shortening	1 16-ounce can apricots
1 cup brown sugar,	(other fruit may be
packed	substituted)

☞ Melt shortening in heavy frying pan, 10 or 11 inches in diameter, and spread the brown sugar evenly over the bottom of the pan. Cover the sugar with well-drained fruit. Set aside while making batter below.

Batter for cake:

3 eggs, separated	1 cup flour
1 cup sugar	1 teaspoon baking powder
5 tablespoons apricot juice	

☞ Add sugar to beaten egg yolks. Stir in apricot juice and flour which has been sifted with baking powder. Fold in beaten egg whites. Pour this batter over mixture in frying pan. Bake in a 375° oven for 30 or 40 minutes. When done, turn out on serving plate. Slice and serve with whipped cream.

WHITE FRUIT CAKE

Serves 2 dozen

2¼ cups sugar	1 pound conserved cit-
2 cups butter	ron, chopped fine
4 cups flour	1 pound almonds
2 teaspoons baking	½ pound conserved cher-
powder	ries (red and green)
¼ teaspoon salt	½ pound conserved pine-
½ cup milk	apple, chopped in
1 coconut, grated	small pieces
	16 egg whites

☞ Cream sugar and butter. Sift dry ingredients together and add alternately with milk. Fold in coconut, fruit and almonds. Then fold in whites of eggs beaten stiff.

Line an angel-food tube pan with greased heavy wax paper. Pour mixture into pan and bake in moderate oven (325°) for 1¾ hours, or until done.

SEVEN-LAYER CHOCOLATE FROSTED CAKE

(TALL, DARK AND RICH)

---

1 cup butter or margarine	3½ teaspoons baking powder
2 cups sugar	½ teaspoon salt
4 large eggs	1 cup milk
3½ cups cake flour	1 teaspoon each vanilla and almond extract

☞ Cream softened butter or margarine thoroughly, then slowly add sugar and cream together until light and fluffy. Add whole eggs one at a time, beating well after each addition. Add sifted dry ingredients alternately with milk to which flavorings have been added. Beat after each addition. Do not over-beat. Preheat oven to 350°. (Bake four layers at once, then three layers.) Grease cake pans and dust with flour. Put about 1 cup batter in each cake pan, spreading it evenly. Layers will be thin. Bake 10 minutes. Remove from oven and immediately turn onto cake rack. Remove from pans. Frost and stack while layers are still warm and second baking is taking place.

RICH CHOCOLATE FROSTING

(MAKE FROSTING FIRST)

---

6 squares unsweetened chocolate	¾ cup evaporated milk
¾ cup butter or margarine	1 teaspoon vanilla
1 tablespoon light corn syrup	6¾ cups sugar, sifted
	1 tablespoon cold water

☞ Melt chocolate and butter over low heat. Add corn syrup. Stir until mixture is melted. Remove from heat and add the evaporated milk and vanilla. Stir until mixture takes on a custard appearance. Add sifted sugar all at once. Do not beat with mixer. Stir until all sugar is absorbed. Keep stirring until it turns to a shiny, creamy frosting. Frosting will thicken slightly as it is being put on cake. Add a little cold water as needed so that it will spread smoothly and retain the glazed look. (This recipe can be used for a four-layer cake also.)

PRIZE CAKE

Makes two 9-inch layers

⅔ cup butterscotch morsels	1 cup sugar
¼ cup water	¼ cup firmly packed brown sugar
2¼ cups sifted flour	½ cup shortening
1 teaspoon salt	3 unbeaten eggs
1 teaspoon baking soda	1 cup buttermilk or sour milk
½ teaspoon double-action baking powder	

☞ Melt butterscotch morsels in water in saucepan. Cool. Sift flour with salt, soda and baking powder; set aside. Add sugar and brown sugar gradually to shortening, creaming well. Blend in eggs, beating well after each. Add butterscotch morsels; mix well. Add dry ingredients alternately with buttermilk, beginning and ending with dry ingredients. Blend well after each addition. (With mixer, use a low speed.) Turn into two 9-inch round layer pans, well greased and lightly floured on bottom. Bake at 375° for 30 to 35 minutes. Cool; spread butterscotch filling between layers and on top to within ½ inch of edge. Frost sides and top edge with seafoam frosting (page 146) or whipped cream.

LACE COOKIES

Makes 24 cookies

½ cup butter	1 tablespoon flour,
⅔ cup almonds (ground)	rounded
dash salt	2 tablespoons milk
½ cup sugar	

☞ Melt butter in skillet. Add remaining ingredients, except milk. Stir over heat until sugar melts. Add milk and blend. Drop by teaspoon on well-greased and floured cookie sheet. Bake in 325° oven for 10 minutes. Watch carefully.

SEAFOAM FROSTING

⅓ cup sugar	1 tablespoon corn syrup
⅓ cup brown sugar, packed	1 egg white
	¼ teaspoon cream of tartar
⅓ cup water	

☞ Combine first 4 ingredients in saucepan. Cook until a little syrup dropped in cold water forms soft ball (236°). Meanwhile, beat egg white with cream of tartar until stiff peaks form. Add syrup to egg white in slow, steady stream, beating constantly until thick enough to spread.

LADY BALTIMORE CAKE

Makes 3 layers

---

1 cup butter	1 teaspoon vanilla
2 cups sugar	2 teaspoons baking powder
1 cup milk	
3½ cups flour	6 stiffly beaten egg whites

☞ Cream butter and sugar. Add milk, flour, vanilla, and baking powder, then fold in the beaten egg whites. Bake in 3 layers 20 to 25 minutes at 400°. Let cool.

Beat 2 egg whites very stiff. Add very gradually 1½ cups powdered sugar, 1 tablespoon at a time. Add 1 cup chopped raisins (which have been soaked 10 minutes in hot water), 1 cup chopped nuts, ¾ cup sliced maraschino cherries. Spread this filling between layers.

Then cover cake with following butter icing: ½ stick soft butter, add 2 cups of powdered sugar and 1 teaspoon vanilla. Add just enough milk to cream and spread. Cover entire cake.

FRUIT-NUT FROSTING

2 cups sugar	1 teaspoon vanilla
¾ cup water	¼ cup candied cherries
¼ teaspoon cream of tar-	¼ cup seedless raisins
tar	½ cup California wal-
dash salt	nuts, chopped
2 egg whites, beaten	
stiff	

☞ Cook sugar, water, cream of tartar, and salt over low heat, stirring until sugar dissolves, and mixture comes to soft-ball stage. Gradually add hot syrup to egg whites, beating constantly. Add vanilla and beat until consistency of frosting is right for spreading. Stir fruit and nuts into frosting.

BUSY-DAY CAKE

Makes 1 layer

1⅔ cups flour	⅓ cup butter or part but-
1 cup sugar	ter
¼ teaspoon salt	1 egg
2½ teaspoons baking	⅔ cup milk
powder	1 teaspoon vanilla

☞ Sift first 4 ingredients together in a mixing bowl. Add shortening, unbeaten egg, milk and flavoring all at once. Beat 2 minutes. Pour into greased and floured 9-inch pan (round or square). Bake at 350° 25 to 35 minutes.

Topping:

   3 *tablespoons butter,*
     melted
   3 *tablespoons brown*
     sugar

   2 *tablespoons cream*
   ½ *cup coconut*

☞ Mix all ingredients together. Spread on cooled cake and place under broiler until it bubbles (5 minutes).

POUNDCAKE

(EASY, BUT VERY GOOD)

Serves 10

---

   1 *cup butter*
   2 *cups sugar*
   2 *cups cake flour*

   5 *eggs*
   4 *teaspoons brandy*

☞ Mix and bake 1 hour at 350°. The brandy gives the cake its distinctive flavor and keeps it moist and fresh for two weeks if kept in the refrigerator. Iced as you wish, or served plain, the cake is equally delicious.

1–2–3–4 CAKE

Makes 3 layers

---

2 cups sugar, sifted
¾ cup butter
4 eggs, separated
1 cup milk
3 cups flour

3 teaspoons baking powder
2 teaspoons vanilla flavoring

☞ Cream sugar and butter together. Add beaten yolks and mix together well. Add milk gradually, beating in well. Sift flour once before measuring and twice after measuring, adding baking powder on last sifting. Add flour gradually and beat in. Add flavoring. Fold in stiffly beaten egg whites. Pour into buttered cake pans.

Bake in 350° oven about 15 to 20 minutes. This is a good old tested basic yellow cake on which any kind of desired icing can be spread.

OLD-FASHIONED

STRAWBERRY SHORTCAKE

Serves 8

---

2 cups flour
4 tablespoons Crisco or
margarine
5 tablespoons sugar

2½ teaspoons baking powder
whipping cream

☞ Using hands, mix first 4 ingredients in bowl. Add enough cream to make stiff batter. Shape dough into small round tea cakes. Bake on greased cookie sheet in 400° oven until brown. Serve with sweetened strawberries and whipped cream.

CHEWY CHOCOLATE BROWNIES

Makes 2 dozen

2 *squares unsweetened chocolate*	¼ *teaspoon vanilla*
¼ *cup melted butter*	½ *cup flour*
1 *cup sugar*	½ *cup nuts, chopped*
2 *eggs, unbeaten*	¼ *teaspoon salt*

☞ Melt chocolate and butter together. Remove from heat and add sugar, eggs, beating well. Add other ingredients and beat well. Pour into greased pan and spread. Bake in moderate oven (350°) for 25 to 30 minutes.

CHOCOLATE FLUFF FROSTING

4 *tablespoons butter*	3 *squares unsweetened chocolate, melted*
1½ *cups sifted confectioners' sugar*	¼ *teaspoon salt*
1 *teaspoon vanilla*	2 *egg whites*

☞ Cream butter; add ¾ cup sugar and blend. Add vanilla, melted chocolate and salt. Beat egg whites until stiff, but not dry. Add ¾ cup sugar, 2 tablespoons at a time, beating after each addition, until blended. Continue beating until mixture will stand in peaks. Add to chocolate mixture, folding in gently, but thoroughly.

7 MINUTE ICING

2 egg whites	1¼ cups white sugar
¼ cup brown sugar	5 tablespoons water

☞ Mix well in top of double boiler over boiling water. Heat and beat for 7 minutes with electric beater. Use one-half recipe for single cake.

CARAMEL ICING

1¼ cups brown sugar	2 egg whites, beaten stiff
⅓ cup water	1 teaspoon vanilla
¼ cup white (granulated) sugar	½ cup chopped nuts

☞ Combine brown sugar, water, and white sugar in a saucepan and boil over medium heat until mixture spins a thread. Remove immediately from heat and pour slowly over beaten egg whites, beating constantly. Set bowl in pan of hot water on stove and continue beating vigorously until icing will form stiff peaks. Remove from stove and stir in vanilla and nuts. Spread on cake.

SNICKERDOODLES

Makes 5 dozen

½ cup shortening	1 teaspoon baking soda
1½ cups sugar	½ teaspoon salt
2 eggs	2 tablespoons sugar
2¾ cups sifted flour	2 tablespoons cinnamon
2 teaspoons cream of tartar	

☞ Preheat oven to 400°. Mix shortening, sugar and eggs thoroughly. Sift together and stir in dry ingredients, except sugar and cinnamon. Roll into balls the size of small walnuts. Roll in mixture of sugar and cinnamon. Place about 2 inches apart on ungreased cookie sheet. Bake 8 to 10 minutes until lightly browned. They will puff up at first, then flatten out with crinkled tops.

CARROT COOKIES

Makes 40 cookies

---

1 cup carrots (cooked, mashed and cooled)	2 teaspoons baking powder
¾ cup sugar	½ teaspoon salt
1 cup shortening	1 egg
2 cups flour	⅔ cup nuts

☞ Combine all ingredients. Drop by teaspoon on greased cookie sheet. Bake at 375° for 12 minutes. Frost with icing.

Icing

Mix 1 box confectioners' sugar with juice and grated rind of one orange. Add ⅔ cup chopped nuts. Cover top of each cookie.

DARK SECRETS

Makes 2 dozen

---

3 eggs, unbeaten	1 cup granulated sugar
1 cup black-walnut meats	5 tablespoons flour
1 cup dates, cut fine	1 teaspoon baking powder
2 tablespoons melted butter	½ teaspoon salt

☞ Mix together. Spread into a floured and greased 8″ by 12″ pan and bake 25 minutes at 350° into 1″ by 1½″ strips, remove from baking pan and roll in powdered sugar.

RICH VANILLA WAFERS

Makes 2 to 3 dozen

½ cup butter	¾ cup flour
⅓ cup sugar	1 egg, well beaten
½ teaspoon vanilla	

☞ Cream butter and sugar thoroughly. Add vanilla and flour, then beaten egg. Drop ½ teaspoonful at a time on cookie sheet and spread dough out thin on the sheet with back of spoon. Bake in 375° oven about 12 minutes, or until cookies are a very light brown. These will burn quickly and must be watched.

BEVERAGES

CAFÉ BRÛLOT

Makes about 1 quart

---

1 medium-sized orange	½ cup warm brandy
4 2″ sticks cinnamon	4 cups hot, double-
12 whole cloves	strength coffee
6 cubes sugar	

☞ Cut rind from orange in thin strips; place in chafing dish with cinnamon, cloves and sugar cubes. Pour in warm brandy and light with a match. Stir until flame dies down and sugar is melted. Add coffee. Serve in demitasse cups after dinner.

IRISH COFFEE

☞ Measure water—1 cup water (using regular-size cup) for as many cups as needed. To each cup of water add 1 level teaspoon of sugar, stir and bring to boil. Measure 2 tablespoons coffee for each cup of water. Put coffee in top of drip-type coffee maker. Pour boiling water and sugar through two times. Put ½ jigger of Irish whiskey in each Irish coffee cup. Fill with hot coffee, leaving enough room for ½ inch stiffly whipped cream. Serve at once.

COFFEE SPARKLE

Makes 10 to 12 glasses

| 1 pint vanilla ice cream | 1 quart sparkling water |
| 1 quart cold strong coffee (instant coffee may be used) | |

☞ Beat coffee and ice cream until creamy. Add sparkling water. Pour over ice in tall glasses.

ORANGE JUICE AND SAUTERNE

☞Half fill a glass with orange juice and add sauterne, leaving just enough room for a small measure of ginger ale. Have all ingredients chilled, of course. Serve over ice.

TROPICAL COFFEE FRAPPÉ

Makes 4 servings

☞ Combine 1½ teaspoons instant coffee and 1½ cups cold water. Stir. Add 1 cup canned pineapple juice and 1 pint vanilla ice cream. Beat with a rotary beater or electric blender until smooth and frothy. Pour into tall glasses and garnish each with pineapple kabobs or pineapple sticks topped with a maraschino cherry.

HUMIDITY KILLER IN A TALL GLASS

Makes 5½ cups or 6 servings

1 6-ounce can frozen limeade concentrate	1 can (1 pint, 2 ounces) pineapple juice, chilled
	1 seedless orange

☞ Turn limeade concentrate into a 1½ quart container; add 3 cans cold water and pineapple juice; stir. Slice unpeeled orange; notch edges of rind; cut each slice in half. Fill tall glasses with ice cubes; fill with fruit juice mixture. Put 2 orange half-rounds in each glass.

GOLDEN MINT PUNCH

30 to 35 sprigs mint	2 #2 cans pineapple
2 cups granulated sugar	juice
2 quarts boiling water	1 quart ginger ale
2½ cups lemon juice	1 quart sparkling water
2½ quarts orange juice	

Put mint, sugar and boiling water in saucepan and simmer for 10 minutes. Refrigerate. Strain mint syrup and add remaining ingredients. Top with fresh sprigs of mint.

This recipe can be used as fruit punch without mint.

ORANGE-CRANBERRY FRUIT PUNCH

Makes about 50 cups

2 cups sugar	16 cups cranberry juice,
3 cups water	or red raspberry juice
8 6-ounce cans frozen	(unsweetened)
orange juice	2 cans frozen lemonade
	8 cups sparkling water

Heat sugar and water together until sugar is dissolved. Cool. Add other ingredients.

FROZEN DAIQUIRI

Makes 10 drinks

---

1 can frozen lemonade,
or
½ can lemonade and ½
can limeade

1 can water (use frozen
lemonade can for
measuring liquid)
2 cans white rum
1 small bottle Seven-Up

☞ Mix ingredients together and deep-freeze for at least 24 hours.

EGGNOG

Serves 20 to 30

---

8 eggs, separated
10 heaping tablespoons
sugar
2 quarts milk
⅓ of a fifth each of
blended whiskey,

Puerto Rican rum,
brandy
1 pint whipping cream
pinch salt
nutmeg

☞ Beat egg yolks until very light. Add sugar and beat again. Add milk slowly. Add whiskey, rum and brandy very slowly, stirring constantly. Fold in whipped cream. Beat egg whites with salt and fold in. Sprinkle with nutmeg. Chill.

MENUS
USED
AT
MARYLAND'S
EXECUTIVE
MANSION

Special Dinners

So far I have been writing about the preparation of separate dishes—about recipes. But nobody eats a separate dish. Nobody serves a recipe. Meals of any kind, from the lightest to the most elaborate, are combinations.

In the old days, down on the Eastern Shore of Maryland, the dining table was laden with foods. The meals were very hearty and heavy. It was an ordinary occurrence to start a meal with rich oyster pie, then have four or five different meats, four or five different vegetables, two or three kinds of potatoes. The table groaned with jellies, pickles, chow chow, preserved figs, hot and cold breads, biscuits—and of course the dessert. A staggering array of food!

The meals we serve today are usually more sensible and certainly better for our health. Today's menus consist ordinarily of a soup, fruit cup, or seafood cocktail, one meat with vegetables and a salad. Of course, there is always the dessert and coffee. I must confess that many times my table still groans, but, after all, these are festive occasions and it is fun to sample the variety of foods.

On the following pages I have listed some of the menus I have served here in the Executive Mansion during the last four years.

Early in 1960, while he was campaigning for the Democratic nomination to the Presidency, the then United States Senator from Massachusetts, John F. Kennedy, came to Annapolis and was Governor Tawes' and my guest at dinner.

Here is what I served that day:

Fresh fruit cup

Stuffed baked turkey with   *Fried Maryland oysters*
giblet gravy (p. 50)   *(p. 21)*
Maryland crab meat   *Smithfield ham (p. 54)*
casserole (p. 16)
String bean casserole with cheese sauce (p. 90)
Frozen salad (p. 78)
Hot rolls (p. 102)   *Chow chow (p. 76),*
olives, celery, cranberry
sauce (p. 72)
Ice cream molds, petits fours
Coffee
Nuts, mints

In 1961, Governor Tawes and I had the pleasure of entertaining Mr. and Mrs. Anthony Grover. Mr. Grover is chairman of the great firm of Lloyds of London. On that occasion, I served:

Maryland diamondback terrapin soup (p. 9)
Maryland beaten biscuits (p. 105)
Maryland oven-fried   *Stuffed potatoes (p. 92)*
chicken (p. 41)   *Spinach soufflé (p. 98)*
Maryland deviled crabs
(p. 20)
Salad of avocado, beets and hard-cooked eggs on lettuce
Chow chow (p. 76), olives, celery
Hot rolls (p. 102)
Cantaloupes filled with ice cream balls
Coffee

Sometimes our guests come to us from very different fields of public activity. This was the case when at one dinner we entertained Maryland Congressman and Mrs. Thomas F. Johnson, and cinema actress Ilona Massey and her husband, Mr. Donald Dawson of Washington. My menu on that occasion was as follows·

Fresh fruit cup
Chopped livers on toast
Stuffed baked turkey with   Lima beans
giblet gravy (p. 50)
Cranberry sauce (p. 72)
Pickles, olives, celery
Brandied peaches surrounded with ladyfingers
and topped with whipped cream
Irish coffee (p. 155)

All the dinners mentioned above have been served to our guests in the Governor's Mansion. We also entertain on board the State yacht a good deal, and I have found that the following menu seems to go well with sea air:

Maryland diamondback terrapin soup (p. 9)
Maryland beaten biscuits (p. 105)
Maryland fried chicken   Maryland crab meat cakes
(p. 42)   (p. 16)
Potato salad (p. 80)
Fresh corn on the cob
Broccoli
Hot rolls (p. 102)
Cantaloupes filled with vanilla ice cream
Coffee

Representatives of the press are always welcome visitors at Government House, and in 1961 Governor Tawes and I were happy to entertain the British consul and his wife, The Honorable Mr. Roy Link and Mrs. Link, and Mr. and Mrs. Fred Archibald of Baltimore. Mr. Archibald is the distinguished editor of the Baltimore *American* and the *News-Post*.

We had cocktails with hot hors d'oeuvres in the State Drawing Room. We then went to the Dining Room where we had this dinner:

Terrapin soup (*p. 9*) *and saltines*

Roast tenderloin of beef,   *Scalloped Maryland*
mushroom gravy (*p. 48*)   *oysters* (*p. 24*)

Sweet-potato balls (*p. 93*)

Asparagus, with cheese sauce (*p. 68*)

Dinner rolls (*p. 104*)   *Government House salad* (*p. 81*)

Olives, pickles, celery, currant jelly

Spanish cream (*p. 120*) *and petits fours*

Irish coffee (*p. 155*)   *Nuts and mints*

Another dinner which I have served a number of times, and which seems to please our guests, is this one:

Maryland clam chowder (*p. 12*)

Maryland beaten biscuits (*p. 105*)

Oven-fried Maryland   *Maryland crab meat cakes*
chicken (*p. 41*)   (*p. 16*)

Hashed-brown potatoes

String bean casserole with cheese sauce (*p. 90*)

Hot rolls (*p. 102*)   *Government House salad* (*p. 81*)

Pickles, olives, celery

Charlotte Russe (*p. 116*)

Coffee   *Nuts and mints*

Special Luncheons Served to Maryland Guests

State luncheons are apt to be feminine affairs. Usually, it is to lunch that the Governor and I invite the women's groups that play so important a part in public life today. On a number of occasions we have entertained such organizations on the State yacht, and here are two menus which I have found popular:

Iced clamato juice (a combination of Maryland
tomato and Maryland clam juice)
Chicken salad (p. 45)
Maryland crab meat cakes (p. 16)
Government House salad   Potato chips
(p. 81)   Maryland beaten biscuits
Pickles, olives, spiced   (p. 105)
pears
Ice cream and chocolate cake (p. 143)
Coffee   Nuts and mints

Tomato Juice
Maryland crab meat cakes (p. 16)
Creamed peas in pastry shells
Potato salad (p. 80)
Hot rolls (p. 102)
Ice cream and brownies (p. 149)
Coffee

At a bridge luncheon for fifty women at Government House, I served this menu, which is always nice for ladies:

Fresh fruit cup
Chicken salad (p. 45)
and thin-sliced Smithfield ham (p. 54)
Maryland fried oysters (p. 21)
Potato chips
Maryland beaten biscuits (p. 105)
Olives
Flower ice cream molds and petits fours
Coffee   Nuts and mints

If you would like a less elaborate lunch, cut out the fruit cup and Smithfield ham and have hot rolls instead of Maryland beaten biscuits. In hot weather serve iced coffee or iced tea.

Other Menus

With large dinner groups I have to have a caterer, but whenever I can, I try to cook and serve small dinners (with our own help), and I do part of the cooking myself, so I can serve Maryland's fine foods using the finest old Maryland recipes.

Here are some of the menus I use on these occasions:

HOUSE AND GARDEN
PILGRIMAGE TEA

Orange-cranberry fruit punch (p. 157)
Fancy tea sandwiches   Petits fours
Open faced tea sandwiches and cheese on banana bread (p. 100)
Shrimp spread on crackers   Cream cheese and nut
(p. 2)   spread on brown bread
(p. 5)
Tea   Coffee
Nuts and mints

PRE-INAUGURAL COFFEE HOUR

(About 30 guests)

Smoked turkey open-faced sandwiches
Smithfield ham (p. 54)
Assorted cheeses, relishes, carrot sticks, radishes
Cream biscuits (p. 104)
Hot pecan muffins (p. 106)   Avocado dip (p. 3)
Potato crisps
Coffee or tea
Macaroons   Mints   Fresh-roasted nuts

SUNDAY MORNING BREAKFAST

Grapefruit or orange juice
Pancakes (p. 108) with maple syrup
Eggs, soft fried in butter   Crisp bacon
Jelly
Coffee or tea

SMALL LUNCHEON

Fresh fruit cup
Crab imperial (p. 17)
French-fried potatoes   Tomato aspic
Spoon bread (p. 100)
Pumpkin pie (p. 135)
Coffee or tea

SPECIAL LUNCHEON FOR MEN

Crab soup (p. 11)
Superb stuffed shad (p. 30)
Buttered fresh asparagus   Creamed potatoes au gratin (p. 94)
Tomato salad, topped with cole slaw (p. 87)
Spoon bread (p. 100)
Frozen lemon pie (p. 136)   Coffee or tea

LUNCHEON FOR MEN

Fresh fruit cup
Superb stuffed shad (p. 30)
Baked and stuffed   Fresh chopped kale with crumbs
potatoes (p. 92)   of bacon and shredded hard-
cooked egg
Spoon bread (p. 100)   Tomato salad
Molded strawberry chiffon dessert (p. 119)   Coffee or tea

SUMMER LUNCH

Maryland fried chicken (p. 42)
Waldorf salad (p. 86)   Fresh peas
Hot biscuits (p. 104)   Pickle relish
Iced tea   George Washington apple pie (p. 133)

LUNCH

Tomato juice
Fried oysters (p. 21) garnished with red spiced apple
rings (canned) or sliced cucumbers
Macaroni and cheese   Fresh broccoli
casserole
Hot biscuits (p. 104)   Stuffed pear salad (p. 85)
Snow pudding (p. 125)
Coffee

DINNER

Maryland diamondback terrapin soup (p. 9)
Maryland beaten biscuits (p. 105)
Roast leg of lamb (p. 53) with mint jelly
Condiment tray with olives, tomato wedges and celery
Fresh asparagus with cheese sauce (p. 68)
Hot rolls (p. 102)
Old-fashioned fresh strawberry shortcake
with whipped cream (p. 149)
Coffee or tea

VARIETY SEAFOOD DINNER — MARYLAND STYLE

Oyster stew (p. 23), saltines
Scalloped oysters (p. 24)   Perfect fried soft crabs (p. 17)
Crab salad with tomato   Brussel sprouts
wedges (p. 82)
Assorted relishes   Spoon bread (p. 100)
Fresh fruit cup with lemon ice balls
Coffee or tea

DINNER

Strawberry fruit cup with lemon ice balls
Roast pheasant with dressing (p. 40)—orange sauce
and garnish (p. 71)
Crab meat cakes (p. 16)   Relishes and cranberry
Green tossed salad   jelly
White creamed corn
Hot rolls (p. 102)
Pumpkin pie with whipped cream (p. 135)
Coffee or tea

INAUGURATION DAY
BUFFET DINNER

Tomato juice cocktail
Roast prime ribs of beef (sliced to order)
Small caponette with bing cherry sauce (p. 49)
Hearts of celery, ripe and   Miniature rolls
plain olives   String beans with almonds
Roast potatoes   (p. 89)
Sherbet and fresh fruit served in brandy snifter, garnished
with fresh mint and served with cookies
Coffee   Tea   Pepsi-Cola

DINNER

Fresh crab meat cocktail
Roast wild goose (p. 39) with Smithfield ham (p. 54)
Hominy au gratin (p. 91)   Harvard beets
Creamed spinach
Condiments   Hot rolls (p. 102)
Pumpkin pie (p. 135)
Coffee

FORMAL DINNER

(Given in honor of Admiral of U. S. Naval Academy)

Crab soup (p. 11)

*Chef's fresh fruit salad
(p. 84)*

*Carrot, celery and radish
curls, olives*

*Maryland beaten biscuits
(p. 105)*

*Capon breast, broiled, with Smithfield ham (p. 48)
and orange glacé sauce (p. 71), served on thin toast*

Orange garnish

*Asparagus with cheese
sauce (p. 68)*

*Fluffy baked stuffed po-
tato (p. 92)*

Individual fried oysters (p. 21)

Dinner rolls (p. 104)

Preserved kumquats

*Crème de menthe ice cream parfait (p. 123), vanilla wafers, fancy
mints*

Irish coffee (p. 155), served in drawing room after dinner

SPECIAL DINNER

Fresh fruit cup with lemon ice balls

Cheese sticks

*Broiled boneless chicken breast on Smithfield ham (p. 47)
with mushroom gravy (p. 48)*

Crab meat casserole (p. 16)

*Government House salad
(p. 81)*

Relishes

*Fresh green peas with
mushrooms*

*Sweet potato balls
(p. 93)*

Assorted hot rolls

Peppermint ice cream

Irish coffee (p. 155), served in drawing room after dinner

Salted almonds, mints

SUNDAY DINNER

Shrimp cocktail—saltines
Broiled steak
Baked potato topped with sour cream and crisp bacon crumbs
String beans with sliced almonds (p. 89)
Government House salad (p. 81)
Celery and olives
Crème de menthe ice   Orange cake (p. 140)
cream parfait (p. 123)
Coffee

SUNDAY DINNER

Fresh fruit cup
Roast wild duck, with orange sauce (p. 71)
Water cress greens   Hominy au gratin (p. 91)
Cranberry salad (p. 77)
Olives and celery   Dinner rolls (p. 104)
Applesauce cake (p. 140)
Coffee

DINNER

Fresh fruit cup with lime ice balls
Prime rib roast of beef
Fresh peas with bacon   Fluffy mashed potatoes
crumbs   and brown gravy
Tossed salad—with dressing (p. 65)
Hot rolls (p. 102)   Pumpkin pie, served warm
*   (p. 135)*
Coffee

D I N N E R

Chilled V-8 juice
Broiled steak, with steak sauce (p. 68)
Creamed mushrooms   *Corn pudding (p. 90)*
(p. 94)
Crab imperial (p. 17)
Government House Salad
(p. 81)
Hot bread, sliced and toasted
Relishes
Spanish cream (p. 120)
Coffee   *Salted nuts*

D I N N E R

Fresh fruit cup
Roast tenderloin of beef with mushroom gravy (p. 48)
Fresh peas with tiny onions and bacon crumbs
Celery and olives   *Sweet-potato balls (p. 93)*
Chef's green salad   *Hot rolls (p. 102)*
Old-fashioned strawberry shortcake (p. 149)
Coffee

D I N N E R

Hot cream of tomato soup
Maryland fried chicken (p. 42)
Green peas with tiny   *Sweet-potato and apple*
onions and crisp bacon   *scallop (p. 96)*
crumbs
Relish, olives, pickles
Hot rolls (p. 102)
Lady Baltimore cake (p. 146)
Coffee

SPECIAL DINNER

Maryland diamondback terrapin soup (*p. 9*)
Maryland beaten biscuits (*p. 105*)
Chef's fresh fruit salad (*p. 84*)   *Celery, olives*
Roast pheasant (*p. 40*) *on Smithfield ham* (*p. 54*) *with orange sauce*
(*p. 81*)
Crab meat cakes (*p. 16*)
Buttered whole cauli-   *Baked stuffed potato*
flower   (*p. 92*)
Assorted hot rolls
Chocolate nut pie (*p. 130*)
Irish coffee (*p. 155*), *served in drawing room after dinner*
Mints—salted nuts

DINNER

Crab soup (*p. 11*)
Oven-fried chicken (*p. 41*)
String bean casserole   *Cauliflower* (*whole*), *but-*
(*p. 90*)   *tered*
Stuffed pear salad (*p. 85*)
Hot rolls (*p. 102*)
George Washington apple pie (*p. 133*)
Coffee   *Mints*

Index